More Praise for the Second Edition of *Get Clients Now!*™

"Too many entrepreneurs think the Internet will somehow solve all their marketing problems by magic. *Get Clients Now!*™ provides a marketing plan that seamlessly integrates online and offline promotion in an easy-to-follow system. It's the perfect tool for the savvy business owner to achieve sales and marketing success."
    —Mitch Meyerson, author of *Success Secrets of the Online Marketing Superstars*

"This is a system that works. C.J. Hayden has taken the mystery out of marketing. She has written a book that is easy to read, easy to understand, and most important, easy to follow. . . . In the first 28 days, I added $5,000 to my bottom line! The focus and clarity this program creates is amazing. Anyone trying to grow a business without this book is doing it the hard way."
    —Rachelle Disbennett-Lee, Training Director, International Coach Academy

"*Get Clients Now!*™ proves that successful self-promotion does not have to be pushy, selfish, or manipulative. The newest edition of C.J. Hayden's bestseller will help you create a marketing plan based on building authentic relationships, being of service to others, and marketing techniques that fit your own personality."
    —Caterina Rando, author of *Learn to Power Think*

"Whether you're just starting your business or ready to take it to the next level, *Get Clients Now!*™ provides a clear roadmap to reach your goals. Make sure to follow the day-by-day marketing plan outlined in the book. You'll create endless opportunities to do what you love—and get paid well for it!"
    —Jill Konrath, author of *Selling to Big Companies*

"*Get Clients Now!*™ pioneered the idea of a simple, action-oriented system for professional services marketing. The updated edition provides an even more effective, proven model for 'non-marketers' to get—and stay—in action and build a sustainable business."
    —Steven Van Yoder, author of *Get Slightly Famous*

"If you want your business to have shameless success, you need *Get Clients Now!*™ C.J. Hayden's comprehensive guide to marketing provides all the essential tools a self-employed professional needs to attract an endless stream of clients."
    —Debbie Allen, author of *Confessions of Shameless Self Promoters* and *Skyrocketing Sales*

"Terrific book. The combination of a system filled with how-to wisdom, and a game plan for following it step-by-step all the way to a successful outcome. Get this book, internalize C.J.'s teaching, and you'll find yourself serving a lot more people; thus making a lot more money."
    —Bob Burg, author of *Endless Referrals*

"I have been using C.J. Hayden's *Get Clients Now!*™ system for years, and I know that I wouldn't be where I am today without it. I actually have a waiting list for clients! If you want to attract more clients with less effort, I urge you to buy this book now!"
—Rich Fettke, Master Certified Coach and author of *Extreme Success*

"It's no secret. A successful business requires marketing and self-promotion. If you want a serious dose of marketing medicine, this book is it."
—Bernard Kamoroff, author of *Small Time Operator: How to Start Your Own Business, Keep Your Books, Pay Your Taxes and Stay Out of Trouble*

"Advice that seems simple is actually the most brilliant, and C.J.'s advice *is* brilliant. She has taken the mystification out of marketing, and has truly given you the 'magic formula' in the context of a 28-day program that anyone can follow. Whatever field you're in, if you want more clients, this is the book for you."
—Susan Harrow, author of *Sell Yourself Without Selling Your Soul*

"All too often, I come across business professionals who have great ideas or products but don't have a clue about how to market themselves or sell their products. This is a wonderfully practical handbook that solves the problem . . . an excellent tool for anyone who is interested in expanding their client base with consistent, easy-to-follow steps. I highly recommend it!"
—Tony Alessandra, Ph.D., author of *Collaborative Selling* and *Charisma*

". . . a fantastic book that takes common marketing knowledge to new heights. The simple step-by-step marketing strategies are designed to help any and every small business succeed. No more feeling overwhelmed with your marketing campaign, no more wondering if your initial steps are the right ones, and no more guesswork. Hayden takes you through each step, and helps you develop a plan that is right for you and your business! Excellent!"
—Alyice Edrich, editor-in-chief of *The Dabbling Mum*

". . . presents the two most important elements for a successful marketing program for consultants: an easy, yet structured process to follow, and the motivation to get started and keep at it."
—Rick Freedman, author of *The Internet Consultant*

". . . an efficient, user-friendly, step-by-step program that anyone can customize and follow. It leaves postulating and theorizing to those who want to simply talk about self-promotion and marketing, and pragmatically zeros in on creating the action plan needed to materialize success. I know, because I tried the program to increase my own client base, and it worked."
—Margo Komenar, author of *Electronic Marketing*

"Read this book NOW! Follow C.J. Hayden's program, and see your business expand immediately. Her system works!"
—Jill Lublin, author of *Guerrilla Publicity* and *Networking Magic*

"A brilliant and effective 28-day marketing program for professionals and consultants . . . offering tools that readers can inject into their marketing efforts with renewed energy and fresh enthusiasm, utilize to design enhanced plans of marketing action, and dramatically increase their client base no matter what their area of consultative practice."

—Bookwatch

"I can't begin tell you how excited I am about the *Get Clients Now!*™ program; it absolutely ROCKS! As a professional business coach, I am constantly looking for the best tools and systems to support my clients in building successful practices. By adding *Get Clients Now!*™ to my toolbox, my practice has absolutely exploded!"

—Travis Greenlee, Business Design and Development Coach

". . . shows you all the proven ways of marketing one's business, and helps you figure out which of these apply to you. It made clear to me exactly what I should be doing—no more guessing."

—Karen Frishman, Marketing Consultant

"I have just completed working the *Get Clients Now!*™ Program. . . . I got four new clients, lined up five workshops and two speaking engagements, and had an article written about me in the local paper!"

—Tifin Kutch, CPCC, Life Coach

"The *Get Clients Now!*™ format is the most time-efficient, productive program I have ever seen. . . . Instead of a production of $4,000 a month, I have been able to produce $8,000 and $10,000. . . . I will become a Mary Kay Sales Director August 1, being in the top 2% of the company worldwide."

—Sharon Richman, Mary Kay Beauty Consultant

"It's a perfect way to get in gear . . . a formula that is right on and uncovers every aspect that needs attention. . . ."

—Josiane Feigon, Telemarketing Trainer & Coach

"*Get Clients Now!*™ is a must-own book. . . . Long before I finished reading it as a whole, I had been introduced to ideas which were not so hidden but had never occurred to me as approaches . . . like the pieces of a puzzle after it is assembled, the author takes the confusion out of marketing and provides fuel for success. I highly recommend this book to those seeking an intelligent marketing plan."

—Edward Harris, Web Designer

". . . excellent, realistic, well-researched and documented book. For some 35 years in broadcast marketing, I wrestled daily with the problem of getting new clients, as a salesperson, sales manager, and general manager. Your book would have made my job much easier."

—Oliver W. Hayden, Radio General Manager

"We really like the knowledge and style of *Get Clients Now!*™ We give it to every new employee of our recruiting firm, as an example of the way we want to work."

—Frank Roders, Compagnon Recruiting, The Netherlands

". . . easy to read, well-written, well-organized, and even usability tested. What I mean by that is that it seems like you have gotten a lot of feedback from real users of your system, and then incorporated that feedback to improve the book. To me, as a computer guy, this is the highest complement I can give."

—Peter Linde, Information Technology Consultant

". . . the program is already helping me. Just writing out a plan makes a big difference. Of course a marketing consultant like myself knows that, but recommending it to a client and actually doing it yourself are two very different things."

—Ramona Rea, Marketing Consultant

". . . gives you a step-by-step, day-by-day action plan, which you can tailor-make to suit your personality. You don't have to do things you don't like doing, but you can see where all the activities you like doing fit in terms of effectiveness. I have attracted six new clients since starting the 28-day program, and I'm only halfway through. Fantastic!"

—Nicola Cairncross, Financial Intelligence Coach

". . . one of the most practical books I have ever seen in my entire life. Really nicely paced with all the forms right there, with a good balance of encouragement and insistence. Superb job! I'm using it already. Today was my first day, and a prospect e-mailed me back unsolicited to call me in for an assignment next week. Just as you promised, once we start marketing with commitment, the work just flows in!"

—Gordon Graham, Marketing Consultant

Get **Clients Now!**™

Second Edition

A 28-Day Marketing Program for Professionals, Consultants, and Coaches

C. J. Hayden

AMACOM

American Management Association

New York ■ Atlanta ■ Brussels ■ Chicago ■ Mexico City ■ San Francisco
Shanghai ■ Tokyo ■ Toronto ■ Washington, D. C.

Special discounts on bulk quantities of AMACOM books are available to corporations, professional associations, and other organizations. For details, contact Special Sales Department, AMACOM, a division of American Management Association, 1601 Broadway, New York, NY 10019.
Tel.: 800-250-5308. Fax: 518-891-2372.
Web site: www.amacombooks.org

This publication is designed to provide accurate and authoritative information in regard to the subject matter covered. It is sold with the understanding that the publisher is not engaged in rendering legal, accounting, or other professional service. If legal advice or other expert assistance is required, the services of a competent professional person should be sought.

Get Clients Now!™ is a trademark of C.J. Hayden, San Francisco, California.

Library of Congress Cataloging-in-Publication Data

Hayden, C. J.
Get clients now! : a 28-day marketing program for professionals, consultants, and coaches / C. J. Hayden.—2nd ed.
    p. cm.
    Includes index.
    ISBN-10: 0-8144-7374-1
    ISBN-13: 978-0-8144-7374-0
1. Marketing—Study and teaching. I. Title.

HF5415.H296 2007
658.8—dc22   2006012211

Printing number

20 19 18 17 16 15 14 13 12 11

To my clients, who taught me all I know

Contents

Foreword

The prospect of getting clients—now!—is a delightful concept. It's a noble endeavor for any business; a desired pot of gold at the end of your rainbow.

It is also a tough job, a baffling and daunting task, and a goal not easily reached by the majority of businesses.

For those reasons, it is absolutely crucial that you pursue that goal with all the chips stacked in your favor. In *Get Clients Now!*, C.J. Hayden has stacked those chips for you. They are neatly and generously provided in the upcoming pages—each chip worth far more than its weight in gold.

Unlike the chips in a poker game, these chips entail no risk for you, and if you bet them, you're certain of winning; assured of victory in the game of obtaining clients. Is it easy to win that game? It is not. Is it the fast track to financial success? Often, no. But if you apply the easy-to-follow advice presented here, getting those clients will become a certainty.

Calling a spade a spade, author Hayden starts right out by telling you exactly why you don't have enough clients right now. You may wince when you read her words, but you won't be able to refute them because you'll know in your heart that they are true.

That's the bad news. The good news is that when you complete this book—and even while you're reading it—you'll see how you can reverse this situation and develop a roster of satisfied, long-term, profitable clients.

Sounds good, but where do you start? You'll get the answer to that question pronto. What should you do right this minute to get clients? That, too, is answered in a way that will bestow you with instant enlightenment.

The complex chore of amassing an abundant list of clients is made simple and attainable with the step-by-step plan the author has in store for you. Where were those steps when I was first starting out? They weren't in any books that I read, nor in the advice given to me by well-meaning friends and even mentors.

But here they are, along with exercises to help you establish the momentum you'll need, and a worksheet that will serve as an infallible guide in your quest for clients right now.

C.J. Hayden has created a clear and effective system for you so that your efforts are not helter-skelter. Along with her system, she gives you a veritable treasury of practical ideas and proven tactics—while stomping on the toes of conventional wisdom that may have led you up the garden path to nowhere until now.

As she reveals a new world of glowing possibilities for your business, she shines a light upon many ugly realities that may have been hindering your progress. But you will be impeded no more. You will no longer suffer from a dearth of clients. Your questions will be answered and your path will be illuminated.

Get Clients Now! makes a promise in its title, then gives you the reward of living up to it.

Jay Conrad Levinson
The Father of Guerrilla Marketing
Orlando, Florida

Acknowledgments

There are four souls without whose help this book could not have been written: my life partner "Friendly Dave" Herninko, who provided hot meals, clean clothes, and loving reassurance so I could keep writing; my feline companions Seabiscuit and KimChee, who leapt on my keyboard, shredded my notes, spun my writing chair in circles, and otherwise reminded me not to take myself too seriously; and coaching godmother Laura Whitworth, who gave me the original idea that led to this book.

I wish to also extend my heartfelt thanks to the following people for their generous assistance: the readers of the first edition, who sent me their compliments, complaints, and inspired suggestions; the coaches, consultants, and trainers who have used this system with their clients over the past ten years; my amazing team of supporters at Get Clients Now!—Joan Friedlander, Angee Robertson, and Annelise Zamula; Barbara McDonald of Native Design for her superb illustrations; marketing guru Jay Conrad Levinson for his early and continued encouragement; the marketing and motivation experts who contributed their words of wisdom for the sidebars in this book; literary agent Sheryl Fullerton and AMACOM editor Ellen Kadin for their ongoing support; my sister coaches who supported me in countless ways while this book was being written—Breeze Carlile, Margo Komenar, Caterina Rando, and Cat Williford; and all the gang at Come 'n' Get It—you know who you are.

Introduction

"The significant problems we face cannot be solved at the level of thinking that created them."

—Albert Einstein

If you are ready to get clients *now*, you have come to the right place. Get Clients Now! is a complete marketing and sales system for consultants, coaches, and anyone who markets a professional services business. This book contains a 28-day program for sales and marketing success. It has all the tools you need to get your marketing efforts unstuck, make an effective action plan, and start getting clients.

In this new edition, you'll find the latest Internet marketing strategies for professionals, an even stronger emphasis on relationship marketing, new contributions from experts in marketing and motivation, and numerous improvements suggested by the thousands of readers who have made Get Clients Now! their sales and marketing bible.

It's easy to think that there is some hidden secret to successful marketing and sales. When you consider all the books you could read, seminars you could take, or consultants you could hire, it makes the process of learning how to market yourself seem huge, mysterious, or even terrifying. But in fact there is a simple answer to all your marketing and sales problems, and it's right here in this book. *The magic formula for professional services marketing and sales is choosing a set of simple, effective things to do, and doing them consistently.* The Get Clients Now! system will enable you to do just that.

Who Should Use This Book

Get Clients Now! is the ideal sales and marketing tool for almost any professional services provider. Some of the many professionals who will benefit are: accountants, attorneys, architects, bodyworkers, chiropractors, coaches, computer professionals, consultants, counselors, designers, engineers, financial planners, freelancers, health practitioners, insurance brokers, photographers, real estate agents, recruiters, speakers, therapists, trainers, and writers. Whether you are a professional marketing your own services or you have business development responsibilities for your firm, this book will provide you with a proven system for finding clients.

The Get Clients Now! system is designed to help you market and sell professional services to either individual consumers or to businesses and organizations. If your service business also markets products, this book may not be a complete solution. You may need other references to help answer questions about which marketing approaches are best for the product component of your business. But for creating a customized marketing plan to sell your services or those of your firm, you won't need to look beyond this book.

How to Use This Book

Get Clients Now! uses a cookbook model to help you create a sales and marketing action plan. First, you will discover the Success Ingredients that are missing from your current marketing and sales activities. Then you will choose from the Action Plan Menu the specific courses of action you should take. Detailed recipes for the recommended tactics and tools are provided to help you successfully implement your plan.

You will get the most value from this book if you commit from the outset to completing the exercises as you go. Just reading the information presented here will be helpful, but where marketing is concerned, more learning is rarely enough to do the trick. You need to choose a direction, take action, and keep moving forward in order to succeed.

Once your action plan is designed, the 28-day program will put your ideas into action immediately. Many people who have used the program report improved results within just a few days. You can use the program quite successfully by yourself; or to make it even more powerful, team up with a business buddy, action group, or personal coach.

For additional resources on any of the topics discussed in the book, to download blank copies of the Get Clients Now! worksheets, or to find a buddy, group, or coach to help you work the program, please visit the book's companion website at www.getclientsnow.com.

C.J. Hayden, MCC
San Francisco, California

"Here is Edward Bear coming downstairs now, bump, bump, bump on the back of his head behind Christopher Robin. It is, as far as he knows, the only way of coming down stairs, but sometimes he feels that there really is another way, if only he could stop bumping for a moment and think of it."

—A.A. Milne, *Winnie-the-Pooh*

Part I

The Setup

Chapter 1

What Really Works? Effective Marketing Strategies

"If you have built castles in the air, your work need not be lost; that is where they should be. Now put the foundations under them."
—Henry David Thoreau

Marketing Made Simple

Marketing is telling people what you do, over and over. There are many ways of telling people—in person, in writing, through the media, on the Web, by phone—but you do have to *tell* them. You can't just wait for the phone to start ringing. You have to tell them over and over. According to the market research firm Yankelovich, Inc., the average American sees or hears up to 5,000 marketing messages per day. Where is your message in all that communication? What will make others remember you if they hear about you only once?

Getting prospective clients to hear what you have to offer and re-member you until they need your service can seem like an enormous challenge. So how do people in your line of work—consulting, coaching, and other professional services—get clients? Ask any successful businessperson that question, and this is what you will hear: "Refer-rals." "Networking." "Making contacts and following up." "Word of mouth."

It's simple stuff; you probably already knew the answers. So why don't you have all the clients you need? If you're like most other first-time users of the Get Clients Now! system, one or all of the following reasons will sound familiar:

- *You can't decide where to begin.* Marketing your business seems like an overwhelming project. There are so many ideas to consider and so many choices to make, and you want to make sure you are doing it right. So you worry about how best to spend your time and money. Struck by "analysis paralysis," you start and stop, sit and stew, or just do nothing.

- *You aren't sure how to put the pieces together.* You think you should be making cold calls but wonder if you need to finish your website first. You suspect it might be time to develop some new leads, but what about those follow-up calls you've been meaning to make? You wonder if all the networking will ever pay off, and whether that speaking engagement will really generate any clients. You don't have a system, a program, or a plan.

- *You can't stay motivated.* Even when you know exactly what you need to do, often you just don't do it. With no boss looking over your shoulder, it's too easy to avoid marketing and sales. When you don't see immediate results, you get discouraged. When someone rejects your sales pitch, it's hard not to take it personally. It's so tempting just to wait for the phone to ring, and blame your lack of business on the economy, the weather, or the time of year.

If any or all of these obstacles have stopped you in your tracks, you are not alone. People who market professional services rarely fail due to lack of information about effective sales and marketing techniques. They fail because they don't use the information that is right at their fingertips. This is why the Get Clients Now! system works; it provides both a structure and a tool kit to turn your marketing goals and ideas into productive action—and it helps eliminate the roadblocks.

How the Program Works

Get Clients Now! breaks down the marketing and sales process into a series of simple steps so you will know exactly where to begin to get clients today. It organizes the steps into a proven system built around three powerful elements: effective, personalized marketing strategies; an action-oriented, 28-day program; and suggestions for managing the fear, resistance, and procrastination that may hinder your marketing efforts. The program shows you how all the pieces of the sales and marketing puzzle fit together: what to do, when to do it, and how to measure your results.

Designing and implementing a successful sales and marketing cam-

Marketing is a System, Not an Event

"Small business marketers love the chase," declares John Jantsch, a marketing coach and author of *Duct Tape Marketing* (Thomas Nelson, 2006). "They love a new-fangled way to make the phone ring. But they often think of a marketing promotion as a single event. It's precisely this view of marketing that holds most small businesses back. They fall prey to the 'marketing idea of the week' and never fully explore what it takes to create and build a completely functioning, consistently performing, marketing system.

"Small business owners have no problem thinking systems when it comes to say, accounting or hiring. When it comes to marketing though, all bets are off. It's as if they are waiting for magic fairy dust to fall upon them with the next great marketing innovation.

"Effective marketing is little more than creating and operating an effective marketing system. When I use the word system I mean several things: 1) the system is documented; you can't have a system unless you write it down, 2) the system is built on sound marketing principles, and 3) you constantly measure, innovate, and refine the system.

"Once you have spent the time and energy to create a plan, you need to commit your plan to a marketing calendar and then allocate the money it will take to implement your plan. When you create a calendar it is much more likely that you will look at the tasks like a 'to-do' list. So, instead of worrying that you should do more marketing, you simply scratch each item off your list and plan for the next. It's an amazingly simple but effective device."

John Jantsch
www.ducttapemarketing.com

paign is a lot like cooking a nutritious meal. When you are cooking, you need to decide what's on the menu, shop for ingredients, and make sure your food choices combine to make a healthful diet. In the first five chapters of this book, you will be guided to select a regular menu of marketing activities that fit your personal tastes, prepare the essential ingredients for sales and marketing success, and evaluate your choices to create a balanced marketing approach.

When your personal marketing action plan is ready for consumption, you'll begin the 28-day program. You'll start each day with a specific list of things to do and get daily advice for working through internal and external barriers to effective action.

To make the best use of this program, you should read Chapters 1 through 5 in sequence, completing the exercises as you go. When you are ready to begin the 28-day program, start reading Chapter 6, one section per day. Two rest days per week are built into the program. Chapters 7 through 10 contain essential marketing "recipes." You can use these for reference while you are designing your action plan, or for help in implementing your plan as you go. Each of these chapters covers one stage of the Universal Marketing Cycle that you will learn about in Chapter 2. You will choose a single stage to focus on during the program and will need to read only the chapter that pertains to the stage you select.

By making this a 28-day program, does that mean you will find all the clients you need in twenty-eight days? In some cases, yes. Since 1995, when this program first became available, many Get Clients Now! participants have landed as many clients as they could handle in less than twenty-eight days. But because everyone's situation and starting place is different, your immediate results may not be what you had hoped. You may choose to keep going with the program for a second twenty-eight days to further improve your sales. That's okay; the program is designed with this intention.

After completing the program, you may choose to repeat it using the same action plan for another twenty-eight days or begin again starting in Chapter 2 to design a revised plan. Either way, you will continue to benefit from the strategy, focus, and motivation that the system provides.

Key Components of the Program

The Get Clients Now! Action Worksheet is the principal planning tool for designing your personal 28-day program. (See the Completed Action Worksheet in Figure 1-1.) Here are the six components of the program included on the worksheet:

1. *Marketing Strategies*—the two to four strategies you will be using during the month of the program.

2. *Marketing Stage*—the stage of the Universal Marketing Cycle where you are stuck or on which you need more work.

3. *Program Goal*—the goal of your program, that is, the results you plan to achieve in the next twenty-eight days. You will set the goal in Chapter 3.

Figure 1-1 Completed Action Worksheet

GET CLIENTS NOW!™ Action Worksheet

What strategies will you use?

1. DIRECT CONTACT AND FOLLOW-UP	2. NETWORKING AND REFERRAL BUILDING	3. PUBLIC SPEAKING	4. WRITING AND PUBLICITY	5. PROMOTIONAL EVENTS	6. ADVERTISING
☑	☑	☐	☐	☐	☐

Where are you stuck or what needs the most work?

☑ Filling the pipeline   ☐ Following up   ☐ Getting presentations   ☐ Closing sales

How much business do you have now? __11 clients__

How much business do you *really* want? __20 clients__

What would that get you? __pay off my credit cards, take a vacation, feel less stressed__

What is your program goal? __4 new clients by the end of the program__

What will be your reward? __go on a ski weekend__

Success Ingredients	Target Date
1. __market niche definition__	__10/06/06__
2. __10-second introduction__	__10/13/06__
3. __3 networking venues__	__10/20/06__

Daily Actions

1. __Spend 1/2 hour each day on my Success Ingredient project__
2. __Send letters or e-mails to 6 new people each week__
3. __Place warm calls to 2 prospects per day__
4. __Go to 1 networking event each week__
5. __Contact 3 new potential referral partners each week__
6. __Have lunch or coffee with a colleague once per week__
7. __Make 3 message board posts each week__
8. __Send an item of interest to 3 colleagues per week__
9. __Ask for a referral once per day__
10. __Visualize success daily__

Special Permission __I give myself permission to have enough time for everything__

4. *Success Ingredients*—the missing ingredients you need to be successful in your marketing and that you plan to create during the program. You will discover these in Chapter 4.

5. *Daily Actions*—ten specific steps you plan to take on a daily or weekly basis over the next twenty-eight days. You will choose these in Chapter 5.

6. *Special Permission*—the permission you need to grant yourself to be successful in areas where you may have failed in the past. There is more about this in Chapter 5 also.

Getting Help to Make It Happen

By using this program, you are going to add a new level of focus, strategy, and structure to your marketing that will substantially increase your likelihood of success. But you can stack the odds more in your favor by adding some outside help. Here are some of the additional aids that can make your sales and marketing efforts more effective and less stressful:

• *Accountability*. Have someone other than yourself to whom you are accountable—someone who will ask you once or twice a week what you have done so far, and what's next.

• *Perspective*. Get a different point of view on your progress or your challenges. Just hearing your problem restated by another person can give you insight that will help you find a solution. When you are feeling low because you haven't reached your goal yet, it's also great to have someone point out that you are more than halfway there.

• *Support*. It's helpful to have someone else to complain to or celebrate out loud with, someone who cares about your progress. If you are up against a roadblock, grousing about it for a few minutes may be all you need to get back into action. And having someone to share your success with can make it much sweeter.

You could use your spouse, best friend, or business partner to provide this extra help, but the individuals closest to you may not be the best choice. The people in your personal life will not always be thrilled that you plan to spend more time on marketing, and your business associates may tend to sidetrack you with immediate problems or day-to-day management tasks. You may find it more helpful to look for accountability, perspective, and support from someone with more detachment yet who

---

Say It and You'll Do It

"Coaching works for many reasons that overlap and intertwine, but one of the strongest threads in this weave is accountability," contends Laura Whitworth, co-founder of The Coaches Training Institute and co-author of *Co-Active Coaching* (Davies-Black, 1998). "It is often the accountability alone that draws people to coaching. They may be competent and successful in many phases of their lives, but there is one area where they have found they cannot make the changes they want to make alone. They're just not getting it done, and they want the structure of a partnership to help them do the thing that is hard to do.

"How many times in your life have you said you were going to do something, and then not done it because nobody else would know the difference? Just the simple act of telling your plan to another person raises the stakes. On a freezing January morning, you might pull the covers back over your head rather than go to the health club alone. But if you've promised to meet someone there at 7:00 A.M., there is a much better chance you'll actually get your chilly butt out of bed and go."

Laura Whitworth, MCC, CPCC
www.thecoaches.com

---

clearly understands the importance you are placing this month on achieving your marketing goals. The best way to get this extra advantage is from a business buddy, action group, or personal coach.

A *business buddy* is a friend or colleague who also wants help to get into action and stay on track. The two of you assist each other in reaching your goals by setting up a regular check-in, with each of you reporting on progress, announcing successes, and stating challenges. The buddy's job is to listen, celebrate, commiserate, and be a brainstorming partner.

Action groups serve the same function for a group of people who wish to work together. You may be able to find an existing group with a business or marketing focus (sometimes called success teams or mastermind groups) through local periodicals or business organizations. If you would like to be part of a group whose members are all using the Get Clients Now! program, you can find a group to join on the book's companion website, www.getclientsnow.com. Some groups have a professional leader, while others have each member take turns leading.

You can also hire your own *personal coach*, a professional who is trained in assisting people to set and achieve goals. Some coaches specialize in working with entrepreneurs or sales and marketing issues. They may call themselves business coaches, marketing coaches, sales coaches, or success coaches. Ask your friends and colleagues if they have worked with a coach to whom they could refer you, or get a list of coaches familiar with this program from the Get Clients Now! website.

Keep in mind that support from a buddy, group, or coach does not have to involve in-person meetings and travel time. Many groups meet via telephone conference lines or live online chats, and your buddy or coach can work with you by phone or e-mail.

What Works and What Doesn't?

In the Introduction, you learned the first secret of successful professional services marketing: Choose a set of simple, effective things to do, and do them consistently. Here is the second secret: *Marketing a service business is not the same as marketing a product.* Products are tangible; you can see them, touch them, maybe even taste them before you buy. Services are intangible. You can't see them until they are demonstrated. They can't be touched or tasted. Because a service is intangible, until it is performed for you, you have no idea how it will turn out, whether you will like it, or whether it will work for your problem, situation, or opportunity.

Therefore, when you purchase a service for the first time, you must rely on your judgment about the person or organization delivering it. There is an old saying in sales and marketing: "People do business with people they know, like, and trust." If a potential client gets to know you, learns to like you, and believes that he or she can trust you, you probably have a sale. Without your having at least one of those factors in place, getting the business will be an almost impossible task.

Keep this crucial rule in mind as you look at Figure 1-2, Marketing Strategies for Professional Services. This diagram operates on three levels simultaneously. First, it shows the six sales and marketing *strategies* that service providers can use. Second, it rates the strategies in order of *effectiveness*, from direct contact at the top to advertising at the bottom. We'll look at each of these strategies in more detail in the next section, but notice that there is a strong connection between effectiveness and the know-like-and-trust factor. Strategies 1 through 3 are much more likely to create a personal relationship between you and the buyer than strategies 4 through 6. The exact order of the individual strategies on the diagram is unimportant, but the overall effectiveness ranking is critical to making the right choices about marketing. Direct contact and follow-up is an effective strategy all by itself, but advertising alone almost never works to find clients.

The effectiveness of a particular strategy can vary with the situation and your own abilities and preferences. A psychotherapist, for example, might find that direct contact and follow-up with potential clients would be inappropriate, and therefore rely more on networking and referral building. A consultant who dreads public speaking would do well to avoid that strategy and concentrate on writing and publicity instead.

Keep in mind that the effectiveness rating of these strategies shown in the diagram refers specifically to their use in marketing your own professional services or the services of your firm. This is what the Get Clients Now! system is designed to address. If your professional practice also includes product sales as part of a service package or an option for existing clients, rest assured that this diagram is completely relevant to your business. For example, a chiropractor who sells nutritional supplements to his clients or a corporate trainer who suggests that training clients purchase her companion textbook will both find this ranking of strategies to be quite accurate. However, defining appropriate marketing strategies to sell products *separately* from your services—whether in your place of business, by mail order, or over the Web—is outside the scope of this book.

The third level of information shown in Figure 1-2 is the *impact* that each strategy creates: outreach, visibility, and/or credibility. Knowing the impact of a strategy will also help you determine whether to use it. Direct contact and follow-up is an outreach strategy, and networking and referral building is both an outreach and a credibility strategy. Public speaking and writing and publicity have the impact of both visibility and credibility, and promotional events and advertising have only the visibility impact.

Notice also that the impacts themselves have an effectiveness ranking. Outreach strategies are clearly the most effective, and visibility-only strategies are the least. Strategies that combine visibility with credibility are ranked in the middle.

Looking at this diagram for the first time, you may wonder where the Internet fits in. How effective is Internet marketing compared to the six strategies shown here? The answer depends on how you choose to use the Web to market your business. The relative effectiveness of your Internet marketing activities follows exactly the same pattern as any other type of marketing you could choose. So networking online will be more

Figure 1-2 Marketing Strategies for Professional Services

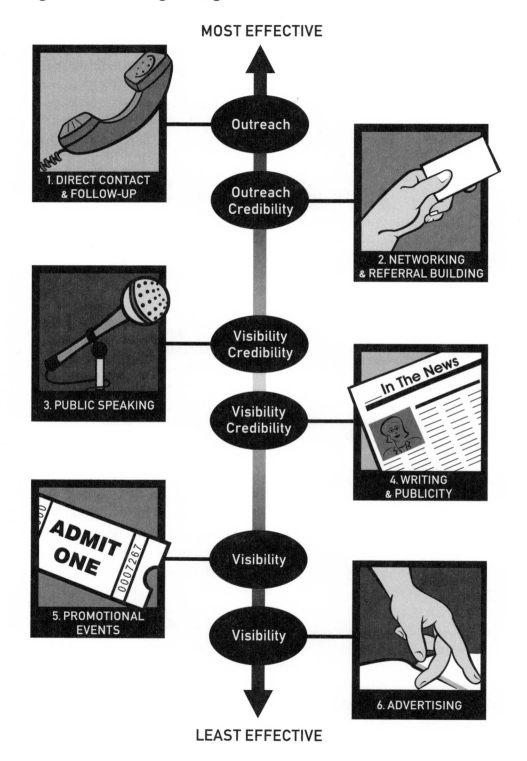

effective than online publicity, for example, and writing for the Web will be more powerful than Web advertising. The Internet is not a marketing strategy in and of itself; it's simply another medium for employing a wide variety of marketing choices.

What Goes into a Strategy?

Think of marketing strategies as the highest-level organizing principle for your marketing and sales activities. When you are trying to decide if you should spend more effort on networking or publicity, for example, remember that networking is ranked as more effective. If you are wondering whether to plunk down a large sum of money for an ad special, ask first what that money would buy if you spent it on promoting yourself as a public speaker.

Every strategy is made up of one or more tactics, or to put it another way, you use specific tactics to execute a chosen strategy. After the definition of each strategy in the following sections is a list of tactics you might use to employ it. And Part III of this book contains detailed marketing recipes that will tell you just how to use these tactics.

The descriptions of marketing strategies that follow will help you begin to consider what activities you will be including in your Get Clients Now! program. Don't worry about selecting specific tactics at this point. Focus on the overall strategies and think about which ones might work best for you.

Strategy: Direct Contact and Follow-Up

Direct contact means making personal contact with a prospective client by phone, in person, or by mail, fax, or e-mail. To get results, your first contact must be truly personal, not a form letter or broadcast e-mail. If you make contact in writing, personalize your communication by addressing it to a specific person and mentioning some issue you know he or she is facing. If you don't do this, you are merely generating direct mail, which is an advertising strategy.

After your initial contact, more impersonal communications, like mailings or e-zines, can become effective follow-up techniques. But for interested prospects, use these tactics as a supplement to personal contact, not a substitute for it.

Note that the marketing strategy of direct contact and follow-up refers to contact with a prospective client. It does not refer to the contact

---

The Name of the Game Is Trust

Marketing consultant and writer Kim Brooks asserts, "If I could write one golden rule of advertising, it would be: consumers hate advertising. I believe that the Internet has finally brought advertising cynicism to a head.

"Consumers are simply tired of all the noise being thrown at them. On buses, billboards, coffee cups, grocery carts, every single page of content on every single website, every page of the newspaper, every 10 minutes on TV . . . there are ads. Consumers have adjusted to this constant barrage: they tune out. But worse than that, they resent it, they distrust it, and they don't buy from it.

"Consumers hate advertising but, luckily, love their friends. You can pummel your Web users with ad after ad with no results. But a single mention of your site from a friend, and he or she will click over faster than you can say 'go.' With cynicism at an all-time high, an overwhelming number of sites, and the endless barrages of banners, users filter out all but the most trusted, most reliable information. They will listen to their friends' recommendations, open their friends' e-mails first, and take their friends' advice over the most cleverly phrased ad message.

"Marketing has now become a trust game. Consumers will listen to sources that they trust, because these are entities that won't yell at them, slick them, or spin them; they will simply pass on relevant, accurate information."

Kim Brooks

---

and follow-up activities you may do with colleagues and others while you are using the strategy of networking and referral building.

Tactics for Direct Contact and Follow-Up

- *Cold Calling.* Call a complete stranger on the phone. Works best if you have reason to believe the person needs your service and you can tell her why with no information from her.

- *Warm Calling.* Call people with whom you have some connection—someone you have met before, someone who has been referred to you, or someone who belongs to a professional or personal community where you are also a member.

- *Lunch or Coffee (with prospects).* An excellent follow-up strategy when your services are expensive or difficult to explain, or the sales cycle is long.

- *In-Person or Phone Appointments.* What many people do to present their service in detail. May lead to a proposal or directly to a sale.

- *Personal Letters and E-Mails.* Send a personal letter by postal mail or e-mail to a hot prospect. This is extremely effective when it is truly personal, not just boilerplate, and is coupled with a follow-up phone call.

- *Announcement Card or Letter.* If you are just starting out, this is a great way to let everyone know what you're doing. Follow up with phone calls.

- *Nice-to-Meet-You Notes.* When you meet someone and collect her business card, send a note. Include marketing literature if it seems appropriate.

- *Sending Articles or Web Links.* Keep in touch with prospects in a nonthreatening way by mailing articles or forwarding links to websites they might find useful.

- *Extending Invitations.* Invite prospects to a meeting or seminar you are planning to go to anyway. It's an excuse to contact them without selling.

- *Reminder Postcards.* When your list of contacts becomes large, do a mailing to remind people you're around. Cards can be easier and cheaper than a newsletter.

- *Newsletters and E-Zines.* A powerful follow-up technique when your service provides valuable information. Use print or e-mail newsletters to show off your expertise and remind people you're available.

- *E-Mail Autoresponders and Broadcasts.* When people make contact via your website, set up an automated sequence of e-mails to provide additional information and follow up with them over time.

 **Strategy: Networking and Referral Building**

Don't limit your picture of what networking means to circulating through a room exchanging business cards. A broader view of networking is creating a pool of contacts from which you can draw clients, referrals, resources, ideas, and information. You can network by phone and online as well as in person. Some of the people you meet through networking will be prospective clients, but you will also make other valuable contacts. Just as you would follow up with a prospect by placing a call or suggesting lunch, you can build your network of colleagues and referral partners in the same way.

You don't have to wait for word of mouth to build in order to start getting referrals. You can seek out potential referral partners by identifying people who are in contact with your target market and getting to know them. After an initial meeting or conversation, you can stay in touch using some of the same tactics as shown for direct contact and follow-up, plus these tactics more specific to networking and referral building.

Tactics for Networking and Referral Building

- *Attending Meetings and Seminars*. One of the best ways to meet people, because they have often come for the purpose of meeting people. Also a good follow-up technique if you keep returning to the same group.

- *Developing Referral Partners*. Seek out people who serve the same clients you do, no matter what their business is. Some people get most of their business from alliances with partners like these.

- *Participating in Online Communities*. Exchanging ideas with the members and readers of e-mail discussion lists, online message boards, social networking sites, and blogs allows you to network without leaving your home or office.

- *Lunch or Coffee (with contacts)*. A good way to get to know referral partners, colleagues, and centers of influence. Your goal is to get them to know, like, and trust you.

- *Staying in Touch with Former Clients*. Your best source of referrals can be people who have already worked with you. Keep in touch and don't be afraid to ask them to refer others.

- *Volunteering and Serving on Committees*. Volunteer your professional services for a high-profile nonprofit to get recognition. Serve your professional community as an officer or committee chair to gain more visibility.

- *Sharing Information and Resources*. Pass along articles or websites of interest, invitations to events, and other ideas and opportunities to the people in your network. They will come to think of you as a resource and refer others to you.

- *Collaborations and Strategic Alliances.* An excellent way for any small business to expand contacts and visibility. Your collaborator may know another whole circle of people.

- *Swapping Contacts.* Exchange leads or past clients with a referral partner in a noncompetitive business. You could even send letters introducing each other.

- *Leads Groups.* A group of people who meet regularly to exchange contacts, leads, and referrals. If you can't find one you like, start your own.

- *Giving Referrals.* One of the best ways to get people to refer you business is to refer business to them. Always be on the lookout for opportunities to refer.

 ## Strategy: Public Speaking

Think of speaking in front of a group as an immensely powerful form of networking. People are much more likely to remember you if you are standing in the front of the room instead of seated in the back. If you are new to public speaking, try starting out small. Volunteer to introduce speakers at an event, or offer your services on a panel. Then gradually work your way up to solo presentations or full-length workshops.

A word of caution about public speaking: look for an already organized group to present to rather than trying to invite your own guests. (That tactic belongs under promotional events.) You may be surprised to find how many civic, business, and professional groups are eagerly seeking free speakers for their meetings.

Tactics for Public Speaking

- *Hosting Meetings.* Any excuse for standing up in front of a group will make you more visible. Serve on a program committee or arrange to make announcements or introductions.

- *Serving on Panels.* An easy way to break into public speaking without having to prepare a whole talk. Let people know you are available to speak on your area of expertise.

- *Making Presentations.* Every meeting or conference needs speakers. Most of them are people like you, speaking for free to promote their business. It gets you both visibility and credibility.

The World's Oldest Yellow Pages

"'No room at the inn! Could you recommend a barn, perhaps, with a manger?' Does that story sound familiar?" asks Susan RoAne, keynote speaker and author of *How to Work a Room* (Quill, 2000) and *How to Create Your Own Luck* (Wiley, 2004). Susan reminds us, "As far back as Biblical times, people have relied on who they know for information and referrals. That is the way we find summer camps for our children, auto mechanics, dentists, good restaurants, and countless other goods and services in our lives. The Yellow Pages are a wonderful resource, but would you use them to identify a cardiologist?

"Networking for word-of-mouth advice and personal referrals is a timesaving and an 'aggravation management' technique to get recommendations for what we need. We have been exchanging those recommendations and sharing resources since Eve offered Adam an apple in the Garden of Eden. It is how the world works—and has, since the beginning of time."

Susan RoAne
www.susanroane.com

- *Virtual Speaking.* Many speaking opportunities exist on webinars, teleseminars, and online chats sponsored by associations, vendors, and professional schools. You can speak to an international audience without traveling.

- *Giving Classes or Workshops.* If you really enjoy speaking or teaching, this is an effective way to expose prospective clients to your expertise. If they like you, they will want more of you.

 Strategy: Writing and Publicity

Writing articles, a column, or a blog about your specialty is an excellent way to gain visibility and credibility you couldn't manage otherwise. If you have never been published before, newsletters, e-zines, and many websites are good places to get your first exposure. Once you have had a few items published, you can graduate to larger publications. Don't rule out these tactics if you're not a good writer. A ghost writer or professional editor can help turn your words into publishable prose.

Getting interviewed by the media can be a bit harder, but you can start small here as well. Small town newspapers like to profile local experts. If you live in a large city, try your neighborhood paper. When approaching the media, always remember that you need to provide them with a story. Tell the editor or producer exactly why their readers will be interested in what you have to say. Tie-ins with holidays or current events are often a good excuse to make contact.

Be aware that unless your piece appears on the front page of the *New York Times*, you shouldn't expect a deluge of phone calls and Web traffic. You are more likely to receive congratulations from people you already know than to hear from a flock of new prospects. Writing and publicity techniques are better for steadily building your credibility and name recognition than for filling your marketing pipeline all at once. An added benefit of these techniques, though, is that you can add the resulting clippings to your marketing kit or display links to them on your website.

Tactics for Writing and Publicity

- *Writing Articles or Tips.* When you publish an article or brief tip in print or on the Web, people not only read it and contact you; you can also send it to your mailing list for follow-up, link to it on your website, and use it in your marketing kit.

- *Reprinting Previously Written Articles.* Get more mileage out of each article you write by finding as many publications and websites as possible to publish it.

- *Writing a Column.* If you appear regularly in the same publication or site, people who read your column will remember you and think of you as an expert.

- *Publishing a Blog.* Making regular updates to a blog can prove your expertise, keep you in touch with prospects, and attract new people to your pipeline.

- *Being Quoted by the Media.* You can make this happen by writing to journalists or bloggers when you see your area of expertise being discussed. Next time, they may contact you for a quote or refer to your work.

- *Having Stories Published About You.* Send a press release about your work, opinions, or achievements to editors that cover your area. Or find a freelance writer in your field, and let her know how interesting you are.

- *Getting Others to Link to Your Website.* Ask other websites aimed at your target market to link to your site. If you post helpful articles, useful tools, and other free resources there, many site owners will be happy to link to you.

- *Being Interviewed on Broadcast Media.* Pitch yourself to producers as a fascinating subject for radio, TV, or Web broadcast interviews. Once you have appeared in just one media outlet, many others will be eager to have you as a guest.

Strategy: Promotional Events

Putting on a show, or being part of someone else's, is a time-honored way of attracting customer attention. Participating in a trade show, or co-sponsoring a fund raiser, can put you in direct contact with potential clients, and bring you an audience you couldn't afford to reach alone. But look out for the cost! Buying a booth, setting up a display, and distributing literature to hundreds of people, or even more, can be extremely expensive. Try evaluating the cost per head of each solid lead you expect the event to generate, and see if you couldn't beat that price by using some other marketing method.

If you want to try producing your own event, such as a workshop or reception, figure out how much it will cost you to bring each person to the door, and see if the expected business will be worth the expense. Publicizing events like this can require a substantial outlay for mailings and advertising. Look to see what the result might be if you spent the same amount of time and money on generating business through other strategies.

Tactics for Promotional Events

- *Trade Shows.* Booths at big shows can be very expensive, but many associations put on more affordable tabletop expos. Trade shows are better for collecting leads than for closing sales.

- *Free Demonstrations or Workshops.* Offer a free demonstration or low-cost workshop to your hottest prospects. It works like public speaking, but you control the invitations.

- *Virtual Events.* Offering a workshop by teleseminar or a demonstration via Web conferencing will allow you to invite prospects from around the world.

Your Parents Love You, But Who Else?

"Publicity markets your services more effectively than advertising . . . or your parents," says Susan Harrow, media coach and author of *Sell Yourself Without Selling Your Soul* (HarperCollins, 2002). "Your parents love you. They think you are the best thing that ever walked this earth. And they're right. They're also biased. And everyone knows that. So when they say great things about you to anyone who will listen, those people's eyes tend to get that opaque and uninterested glaze. A similar thing happens when an audience reads or sees advertisements. Even when someone is looking for a specific product or service, they know that anyone who has the money can buy space to plug their products.

"When a journalist writes a story about you or your business, you are already one step ahead of those people who choose advertising. Why? You have literally and symbolically passed through a gatekeeper—the editor or producer who has judged that you have something of value for his audience.

"People perceive a journalist or producer as an unbiased source of information. The person who is included in an article or is on a radio or TV show has passed through a journalist's or producer's screen. We credit the media with knowing a good story when they see one. You can't buy the kind of prestige that puts you on the front page of a major newspaper."

Susan Harrow
www.prsecrets.com

- *Open House or Reception*. Find an excuse to throw a party, and invite prospects and referral partners. People who don't return your calls may surprise you by showing up here.

- *Co-Sponsored Events*. Co-sponsoring a workshop, symposium, or fund raiser with a nonprofit will attract clients who support the cause. Collaborating with a colleague on an event will maximize your resources and extend your reach.

- *Networking Lunch, Breakfast, or Mixer.* Invite clients, prospects, and referral partners to meet each other for their own benefit. Tell everyone to bring a guest.

 **Strategy: Advertising**

Many consultants, coaches, and other professionals have found advertising of any kind to be quite ineffective at filling their marketing pipeline with paying clients. Remember the know-like-and-trust factor: ads don't allow clients to get to know you personally. This doesn't mean that advertising should be completely eliminated as a possible strategy. A website, for example, is an advertising tool that most businesses will want to have.

For some professional service providers, print or Web advertising can be a reliable source of leads. An ad in the Yellow Pages, for example, can bring new inquiries to a professional who people often seek in an emergency, like a dentist; need only rarely, like a resume writer; or prefer to locate privately, such as a psychotherapist. For professionals who offer date-dependent programs like seminars and group work, advertising via direct mail, flyers, or calendar listings is often necessary. But in most cases, advertising alone rarely generates business; it must be coupled with direct contact and follow-up tactics in order for it to pay off.

To determine what role advertising should play in your marketing, ask yourself this question: "How do clients usually select a service like mine?" If your immediate answer is "by referral," you will probably find most advertising to be a waste of money. But if your clients often do make their buying decision from advertising, you may need to consider some forms of it.

Take a look at your competition and see where and how they are advertising. Ask questions of your colleagues about what type of advertising has and hasn't worked for them. Advertising can be an expensive proposition. Evaluate the potential return on any advertising investment. How many clients will it bring you before it pays for itself? And is there some other more effective way you could spend the same money?

On the Web, for example, you might choose to have a website for your business but not to invest additional funds in advertising with pay-per-click ads or paid-inclusion directories. You can instead use some of the other approaches discussed in this chapter to attract traffic to your site. Strategies like public speaking or writing and publicity are more likely to generate Web visitors that quickly turn into clients. You'll have a much harder time closing sales with people who get to your site by clicking on an ad.

Tactics for Advertising

- *Newspaper or Magazine Classifieds.* The more targeted your ad, the better. Ask for an immediate response from readers, perhaps with a special offer. Track every response you get to see how well the ad is working.

- *Display Ads in Newspapers, Magazines, and Trade Journals.* Ads like these are typically more for visibility than direct response. You usually need a big budget, and repeat advertising, to make them work.

- *Yellow Pages.* Works well only if your service is something people will look for there, and your ad is one of the most noticeable. Don't waste money on a small ad in a big category.

- *Other Print Directories.* Follow the same rules as with the Yellow Pages, plus check into distribution before you buy. Will your potential clients actually see this directory?

- *Professional Directories.* Will get you business only if people actually use it, but consider credibility also. If a certain directory is the official source for an industry, you probably want to be in it.

- *Event or Conference Programs.* Another visibility booster that may need a big budget. Works best if people who already know you will notice the ad.

- *Website.* A website by itself is a tool rather than a complete strategy. You may decide to use your site primarily as an online brochure: sending visitors to it with other strategies rather than expecting it to attract traffic on its own.

- *Search Engine Positioning.* The lowest-cost way to attract traffic to your website can be to get your site ranked more highly in search engines. Building a site that includes a high density of relevant search terms in its text and offers extra value with articles and resource links will improve your rank.

- *Web Directories.* Listing your site in major directories, or specialized ones used by your clients, can increase your visibility. Some directories charge a fee to include your listing; others are free.

- *Pay-per-Click Advertising.* You pay for these online ads each time someone clicks on one to visit your site. Costs can add up quickly, so evaluate your potential return carefully before choosing this option.

- *Banner Ads.* For these online display ads on websites and in e-zines, you'll typically pay a flat fee for a length of time or per issue. Be sure you know the number of visitors who will see your ad before you buy.

- *Bulk E-Mail.* Sending bulk e-mail to market your professional services is probably the least effective advertising tactic you could choose, and the most likely to annoy your prospects.

- *Direct Mail.* Postal mass mailings have nowhere near the impact of personal letters, and are often a waste of money. Consider narrowing your target group and using direct contact tactics instead.

- *Flyer Distribution.* Flyers are cheaper than throwing brochures around and can be used to develop interest with a targeted group. They work best if a limited time offer is included.

- *Radio or TV Ads.* You need a substantial budget to go this route. Ads must be repeated to have any effect. If you do this, get professional help in scripting and producing your ad.

- *Billboards.* For professional services? Well, people have done it. You can probably find better ways to spend the money . . . like one of the other tactics already mentioned.

Making Your First Selection

After reading this overview of potential marketing strategies and tactics, you probably have some idea of which strategies you might like to use in your Get Clients Now! program. Consider which two, three, or four strategies you think you would most like to employ. More than four strategies are too many to attempt in a 28-day period, and fewer than two won't give you enough flexibility.

If you're unsure which strategies might be best for you, keep reading. You'll find more guidance on selecting strategies in Chapter 2.

But What About Selling?

In thinking about what marketing strategies to use, it may have occurred to you to ask where selling enters the picture. This is another way in which marketing a service can differ from marketing a product. When you are selling professional services, marketing and sales are not two separate activities that occur at different times; instead, they must be seamlessly integrated. Think about it. If you are talking to someone about what you do, you may think you are networking. But if she expresses an interest in doing business with you, you are instantly in a selling situation.

The exact opposite is equally true: if you make contact with a prospect in order to sell your service, the person may tell you that he isn't

Get Personal About Your Marketing

Tony Alessandra, the author of 14 books, including *Collaborative Selling* (Wiley, 1993) and *Charisma* (Warner Books, 1998), points to experienced salespeople as a powerful model for people selling their own services.

"The successful sales rep seems to just sit back and respond to calls. The orders roll in, and she seems to be getting rich without effort. What we generally don't see are the years she spent building her network, and investing in her personal visibility.

"This successful salesperson is using personal marketing. She's marketing herself just as a company would market a product. Just as it takes time to build brand loyalty, it takes time and hard work for personal marketing to pay off, but it's worth it in the long run. If your best potential clients have been made aware of you in advance of your contact with them, you'll find it much easier to set up an appointment, establish a relationship, and consummate the sale.

"Keep in mind that it's better to work on getting multiple exposures to a smaller target group than to spread your effort and have fewer exposures to more people. Potential clients in your target market should be reading your articles, receiving mail from you, hearing you speak or give a seminar, bumping into you at a social function or trade show, and hearing about you and your expertise from their fellow association members and friends.

"The reason it's so important to invest your time in these methods is that the quality of an incoming lead is almost always better than the lead you get in a cold call. The prospect who calls you has already identified his need for your service, and he's calling to get your help.

"When you effectively use personal marketing, you'll find that little by little, people will start to recognize your name, your company, your product, and your face. Pretty soon the phone will start to ring for you, and your image as an established expert will start to take hold."

Tony Alessandra, Ph.D.
www.alessandra.com

interested but has a colleague who might be. Then you would switch from selling to networking.

The marketing strategy of direct contact and follow-up could also be thought of as personal selling. But it would be misleading to call it that, since in many cases when you make contact, you are not "selling" at all. You may be asking a potential client how her business is going or what she's working on these days. You could be inviting her to your upcoming open house or speaking engagement. The fact is, when you are personally telling a prospect what you do, selling can happen at any point.

So think about everything you do to get clients as being both marketing and sales at the same time. Think about every marketing strategy as a selling strategy, and vice versa.

A Word About Terminology

Before moving on to the next chapter, it might be helpful to review some of the terminology used so far. Up to this point, you have encountered marketing strategies, tactics, and types of impact. Each overall strategy (e.g., direct contact and follow-up) is made up of tactics (e.g., cold calling, warm calling, or personal letters), and has a resulting impact (outreach, visibility, or credibility). In a few pages, you will also learn about stages of the marketing cycle. If you remember the distinctions among these terms and the elements they represent, you will be able to follow the process of building your Get Clients Now! program more easily.

Chapter 2

Where Do You Start? The Marketing and Sales Cycle

"You can't just sit there and wait for people to give you that golden dream; you've got to get out there and make it happen for yourself."
—Diana Ross

The Universal Marketing Cycle

Marketing and sales operates on a predictable cycle, with four separate stages:

1. Filling the Pipeline

2. Following Up

3. Getting Presentations

4. Closing Sales

The activities that take place within each stage of the cycle will vary depending on your business, but the cycle is the same for everyone. Knowing more about how this cycle works will enable you to determine exactly where to focus more time and energy in your marketing.

Figure 2-1 depicts the Universal Marketing Cycle as if it were a water system. At the top are the collection buckets for the prospects, contacts, leads, and referrals with which you are filling the pipeline. On your desk, computer, or favorite handheld device, these will be represented by the names and phone numbers of people and organizations. *Prospects* are people you attract using a visibility strategy, such as publicity or advertising. *Contacts* are people you meet through outreach strategies like networking,

Figure 2-1 The Universal Marketing Cycle

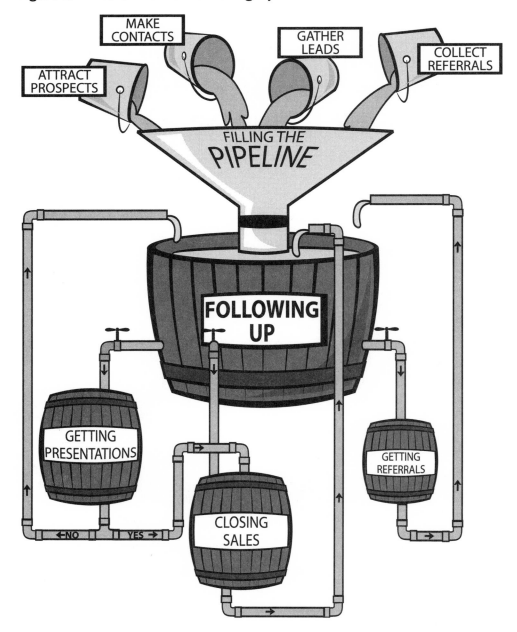

or just in the course of business or life. *Leads* are people you identify through research or hear about from your contacts. And *referrals* are people who are referred to you by contacts, clients, and others.

Don't worry too much about the distinctions among these categories. They are all people in your pipeline.

The marketing pipeline empties into the follow-up pool, which you dip into in order to move potential clients and referral sources further along in the system. Your goal is to keep the follow-up pool constantly circulating, with new prospects entering the pipeline and existing ones flowing into the next stage of the cycle.

The arrows in the bottom half of the diagram indicate the direction of flow. With potential clients, you want to move quickly to getting the presentation. This is where you find out about their needs, tell them more about what you do, and see if there is a match between the two of you. The actual presentation may happen formally or informally, in person, by telephone, or even by e-mail. Some professionals offer a complimentary consultation or sample session as the core of their presentation. When the presentation concludes, you may be ready to ask for the business, or you may need to prepare a detailed proposal first. In some cases, the presentation stage may last 15 minutes, and in others, it can take many months.

Your desired result, though, is always the same: to move prospects forward to closing the sale. If they say yes at the end of the presentation, you have done it. If they say no, back they go into the follow-up pool, where you continue to follow up with them as long as it seems worthwhile. Sometimes follow-up will lead directly to closing the sale after all, and at other times, you may need to make yet another presentation.

When the sale is closed, you begin to serve the client. As you are providing service, and after you complete your service, the client must also return to the follow-up pool. By continuing to follow up with this client, you may close another sale or get referrals.

Some of the people and organizations in your pipeline may never enter the prospect area of the cycle at all. They may be contacts who can be referral sources for you. You must follow up with these people also, regularly reminding them that you are around, thanking them for referrals, and putting them right back in the follow-up pool.

In any of these cases, what follow-up looks like and how often it happens depends on the nature of your business and the type of contact that seems natural for you. Refer to the tactics listed in the previous chapter under direct contact and follow-up. Every one of these is a potential follow-up technique.

To Grow Your Clients, Tend Your Garden

"All roads eventually must lead to follow-up," says Joan Friedlander, a business coach who has facilitated more than twenty Get Clients Now! programs. "It doesn't matter what other strategies you use; if you don't follow up, and do it consistently and continuously, you'll be stuck forever filling the pipeline and never close any sales. I had one client who thought she needed to go out and meet more people in order to build her business. When we probed a bit, she suddenly realized that she had a huge stack of cards in her drawer from all the people she'd already met but never followed up with. Why? Follow-up takes time and effort, and it's not always as exciting as pipeline-filling.

"I often use the metaphor of gardening to help create perspective about the value and importance of following up. When you decide to plant a garden, there are several steps to take before you see results. You plan the space, prepare the soil, buy the seeds or seedlings, plant them, water, fertilize, and weed. Watering, fertilizing, and weeding are like your follow-up activities. They may not be as much fun as planting, but if you don't do them regularly and consistently, you'll have no plants and one ugly plot of land."

Joan Friedlander
www.lifeworkpartners.com

How Does the Cycle Work?

Let's look at two examples. Suppose you are a computer systems consultant who typically works with large corporate clients. At a breakfast meeting of the Association of Information Systems Professionals, you met the director of information technology (IT) in a major corporation. You spoke for a few moments about his company and exchanged business cards. The director is now a contact in your marketing pipeline.

When you returned to your office, you entered his name and other information into the contact management system on your computer and set up an automatic reminder to place a follow-up call the next day. He is now in your follow-up pool.

The next day, the IT director's name and phone number popped up on the reminder list displayed on your computer. You called him, got his voice mail, and left a message reminding him of your meeting, briefly describing the kind of work you do, and suggesting it might be to his benefit if the two of you were to talk. Then you set up another reminder to follow up again three days later.

The IT director did not return your call, so when he popped up on your reminder list again in three days, you placed another call. This time you reached him, but he didn't have time to talk. He did mention, however, that some changes were coming in his company that might indicate a need for your services. With this new information, the IT director is now a prospect rather than just a contact. He is still in the follow-up pool.

You now send the IT director an e-mail, telling him how you could be helpful to him during this upcoming project. You provide a link to your website, referring him to some biographical information about you, a summary of the type of services you provide, and a list of satisfied clients. A week after sending the e-mail, you call him again. After three phone calls over ten days, you once again reach him in person. This time you suggest a meeting, and he agrees to meet next week. He has just moved from the follow-up pool to the presentation stage.

At the presentation, you spend about half the time asking questions and learning about his company and the upcoming project. Then you describe how you can help him, and why you are uniquely qualified to do so. You answer his questions about your background and expertise. At the end of an hour, you ask if he is interested in using you on this project. He asks you to prepare a proposal, outlining what you would do and how much it would cost. You agree, and before leaving you schedule a time with him a week later to go over the proposal in person. At this point, the IT director is still in the presentation stage.

One week later, you meet with him to discuss your completed proposal. You explain what you have written, and the rationale for your process and pricing. After answering his questions about the proposal, you ask if he is ready to sign a contract with you. He tells you he must discuss your proposal with the CEO before making a decision. You make sure he has all the information he needs for that discussion, and offer to be present at the meeting. He declines your offer but tells you he will decide within two weeks. The IT director has now moved from the presentation stage back into the follow-up pool.

Two weeks pass without the IT director's contacting you, so you e-mail him. He replies that the CEO has not yet had time to meet with him and suggests you try back in another couple of weeks. You e-mail again after two more weeks go by, and wonder of wonders, the IT director says the CEO is in favor of hiring you. You ask him when you can get to work, and he suggests you come to a project planning meeting next Monday. Congratulations! You have just closed the sale.

That the entire process took over two months from beginning to end is not unusual. Sales cycles even longer than this are common, whether your clients are big companies or single individuals. Following up is in the center of the Universal Marketing Cycle diagram for a reason: consistent

---

Self-Promotion Serves Your Clients

"You can't be truly successful if you aren't willing to let people know that you, your product, and your services exist," advocates Debbie Allen, motivational speaker and author of *Confessions of Shameless Self-Promoters* (McGraw-Hill, 2005). "If you aren't willing to promote your talents, expertise, and products, others will quickly pass you by. The world is not going to beat a path to your door unless you pave the way. Resenting self-promotion is one of the greatest obstacles to success.

"Those who don't feel comfortable with self-promotion hold a negative belief system around it. They own this negative belief because they don't understand the difference between aggressive promotion and assertive promotion; between ineffective promotion and effective promotion. Yet there is a huge difference!

"Ineffective self-promotion comes across as rude, pushy, boastful, and self-serving. Just as many people who are opposed to it believe it to be true. Yet that is ineffective, and not what I'm suggesting to you.

"Effective self-promotion comes from a different place— a place of caring from your heart. When done effectively, it comes out from a place of passion: a place of help and support first and foremost.

"Effective self-promotion comes across as serving others first, versus ineffective self-promotion that serves the person promoting first.

"When you effectively promote yourself, more prospects will be readily open to doing business with you. They will then return the favor to you in the form of increased sales, profits, success, and wealth."

Debbie Allen
www.debbieallen.com

and persistent follow-up is central to successfully moving a prospect forward to making a sale.

Now for our second example, let's say you are a career coach whose clients are professionals in job transition. You gave a talk entitled "Planning Your Next Career Move" to the Professional Women's Network. At the end of your presentation, you asked for anyone who was interested in finding out more about career coaching to give you a business card. Three women in the audience—Elsa, Mindy, and Dolores—gave you cards. They are now prospects in your marketing pipeline.

The following morning, you stapled each card to a page in your prospects notebook and noted where and when you met these women. You mailed each of them a copy of your brochure with a personal note. In your daily planner, you entered an action item for one week later to place follow-up calls to all three. They are now in your follow-up pool.

Two days later, Elsa called you. She had read your brochure and wanted to find out how much you charge. The moment you picked up the phone, Elsa was in the presentation stage.

You asked Elsa to tell you about her situation and explained how you thought you could help. After making sure she understood what she was getting for her money, you told her your rates, and asked if she wanted to make an appointment. She said yes. You have just closed the sale with Elsa. And of course, five days later, you will still call Mindy and Dolores, who remain in your follow-up pool.

Choosing Where to Focus

The Universal Marketing Cycle is a clever diagnostic tool to help you choose where to focus your marketing efforts. The key to success is narrowing your marketing focus to work with just one stage of the cycle at a time, even when you are following up on many possibilities. Think about your own situation as you review the cycle. Where in the system are you stuck? What stage of your marketing needs the most work:

1. Filling the Pipeline—knowing enough people to contact?

2. Following Up—contacting the people you already know?

3. Getting Presentations—getting from follow-up to presentation?

4. Closing Sales—getting from presentation to sale?

In most businesses, contacting prospective clients directly is one of the primary methods of follow-up, so knowing enough people to contact is an easy test to see if your pipeline is sufficiently full. But if you are in a field where direct solicitation of clients is inappropriate, such as psychotherapy or, in some cases, law, ask yourself if enough people are calling you. Another good test is to imagine you were using a newsletter or e-zine for follow-up. How many people who already know you could you send it to?

Do you already know where you are stuck or need more work? If so, skip ahead to the next section, "What Strategies Should You Use?" If not, try asking yourself some questions.

If you answer yes to the following questions, you need to focus on *filling the pipeline*:

- Are you brand new in business?
- If you sat down to call every lead you currently have, would you be through before lunch?
- Have you personally followed up with every prospect on your list within the past 30 days?
- Are you not contacting the prospects you have because you already know they don't need you or can't afford you?
- Are you in a business where it's inappropriate to contact prospective clients, and you're not getting enough inquiries?

If you answer yes to the following questions, you need to concentrate on *following up*:

- Do you have a drawer full of business cards from people you have met but have not spoken to since?
- Have colleagues handed you leads who you haven't gotten around to calling?
- Are there prospects who said no or didn't return your initial call who you haven't contacted in the past three months?
- Do you have a wide network of personal contacts with whom you never talk business?
- Are there people you haven't been in touch with who inquired about your services in the past, but weren't quite ready or didn't have the funds?

Keep the Pipeline Flowing

Frank Traditi is an executive coach, small business marketing expert, and co-author (with C.J. Hayden) of *Get Hired Now!* (Bay Tree, 2005). "'How do I turn more prospects into clients?'" asks Frank. "That's the burning question asked by nearly every service professional or consultant. Is there a secret code that unlocks the door to success? Not at all. The answer lies in your follow-up.

"Following up is the focal point for all of your sales opportunities. It's why the follow-up bucket is so prominent in the marketing and sales cycle. While you may feel that your services are good enough to sell themselves, it is consistent follow-up that truly moves your prospect from 'maybe' or 'later,' to 'yes.'

"To keep all of your potential client opportunities flowing smoothly in and out of the follow-up pool, make following up a priority. If the sales process has slowed down, it's probably due to lack of follow-up. Try to engage in some form of follow-up activity every day.

"Let go of any fear, uncertainty, or doubt about following up with your prospects. They actually expect your call and want you to help move the relationship forward. Remember to offer value in all your follow-up activities. Every contact with your prospects is a chance to demonstrate your expertise.

"And keep track of your progress. Always know where you are in the sales cycle with each prospect. This will help you move every prospect toward a sale much faster."

Frank Traditi
www.coachfrank.com

If you answer yes to the following questions, you need to work on *getting presentations*:

- Do you follow up with prospective clients consistently, but can't seem to get an initial meeting?

- Do people refuse to take your call, or brush you off quickly when you do get through to them?

Pick What's in Front of You

Robert Middleton has been helping independent professionals become better marketers since 1984. "When helping my clients with their marketing, we'll often be working on how to contact new prospects most effectively," Robert explains. "We'll look at associations, directories, and mailing lists, and discuss the most appropriate ways to get prospects' attention and get in front of them. Then I ask whom they know in their current network of business associates and past clients to contact as well.

"It's not unusual that they have a contact list of several dozen, if not several hundred, people whom they have some business connection with. When I hear this, I suggest they put any cold contacts on a back burner for now, and pay closer attention on how to pick all that 'low hanging fruit.'

"The truth is, you may not need to make as much effort as you thought to generate new clients. They may be closer than you think. Still, you need a plan to contact these people, and make the best of those contacts."

Robert Middleton
www.actionplan.com

- Are all your prospects already working with a competitor—or at least that's what they say?

- Does everyone you contact seem to think what you do is too expensive, will take too much time, or is just not for them?

Finally, if you answer yes to the following questions, it's time to focus on *closing sales*:

- Are you regularly getting to the presentation stage, but don't seem to close enough sales?

- Do your prospects seem to be going through the motions of allowing you to present, but have no serious interest?

- Are you encountering objection after objection that prevents the sale from going through?

No Marketing? No Business!

Stephen Fairley is the author of *Getting Started in Personal and Executive Coaching* (Wiley, 2004) and *Practice Made Perfect* (TLC Business, 2002). Stephen claims, "Most people who start their own professional practices are technicians—the people who really just want to do the actual work of consulting, coaching, law, etc., which is great and necessary. However, technicians typically underestimate the difficulty of the other three essential roles; that is, starting, building, and maintaining a successful practice. They also typically overestimate their ability to market and sell their services.

"Other than the actual decision to start the business, the sales and marketing aspects are the most important function of your business. If there is no sales and marketing, there are no clients to service. If there are no clients, there is no revenue. If there is no revenue, there is no business. It is all a big cycle, and that cycle starts and ends with sales and marketing. To be successful in your professional practice you must accept that you are the chief marketing officer as well as the vice president of sales. There is just no getting around it. If you don't market yourself and sell your ability to help people, you will never get clients."

Stephen Fairley, M.A.
www.businessbuildingcenter.com

- Do you often conclude a presentation and still don't know where the client stands?

What Needs the Most Work?

Now that you know where you are stuck, it's time to choose where you will focus your marketing efforts for the next twenty-eight days. If you think you need work in more than one stage of the Universal Marketing Cycle, start with the first one in the sequence. For example, if you feel stuck on both follow-up and getting presentations, choose follow-up. If you aren't sure where to start, begin with filling the pipeline. And if that's not really where the problem is, you will find out soon enough, and move forward to the right stage anyway. Just be sure to pick only one.

What Strategies Should You Use?

Once you have chosen which stage of the Universal Marketing Cycle to focus on, the next step toward designing your own personal Get Clients Now! program is to determine which of the marketing strategies discussed in Chapter 1 you are going to use for your action plan. The following chart illustrates which strategies are most appropriate to use during each stage.

If you chose . . .   *You should use the strategies . . .*

Filling the Pipeline   1. Direct contact and follow-up

2. Networking and referral building

No more than one or two of the following:

3. Public speaking

4. Writing and publicity

5. Promotional events

6. Advertising

Following Up   1. Direct contact and follow-up

2. Networking and referral building

Getting Presentations   1. Direct contact and follow-up

2. Networking and referral building

No more than one of the following:

3. Public speaking

4. Writing and publicity

5. Promotional events

Closing Sales   1. Direct contact and follow-up

2. Networking and referral building

No more than one of the following:

3. Public speaking

4. Writing and publicity

The strategies recommended for each stage are listed from most to least effective. Direct contact and follow-up plus networking and referral building are considered to be the most effective approaches overall, regardless of which stage you are in. While any of the strategies listed for your stage will work, the ones listed first in each case are most likely to produce results with the least struggle. It's a good idea to employ the most effective strategies, unless there is some reason that a particular strategy won't work well for you. If you are nervous about speaking in public, for example, you might choose writing articles as an alternative to add more credibility to your approach.

What are the best strategies for your situation? Review the marketing strategies you tentatively picked in Chapter 1 against the appropriate strategies for the stage of the Universal Marketing Cycle you are working on. Defining specific marketing strategies to use consistently is one of the most important ways the program will help you to focus your efforts. Therefore, you will need to stick with the strategies you select now for the entire program. Choose at least two, but no more than four, marketing strategies for your 28-day plan now.

Filling Out the Action Worksheet

With your two to four marketing strategies chosen, you are ready to begin filling out your Action Worksheet. A blank worksheet is provided in Figure 2-2. Because you may wish to make changes to your worksheet later or repeat the program after the initial twenty-eight days, make an enlarged photocopy of the blank worksheet, or download a copy at www.getclientsnow.com.

Make your first entries on the worksheet now. Check the boxes that correspond to the marketing strategies you will be using and the stage of the Universal Marketing Cycle where you need the most work. Now let's go on to the next step: setting your sales and marketing goal.

Figure 2-2 Blank Action Worksheet

GET CLIENTS NOW!™ Action Worksheet

What strategies will you use?

1. DIRECT CONTACT AND FOLLOW-UP	2. NETWORKING AND REFERRAL BUILDING	3. PUBLIC SPEAKING	4. WRITING AND PUBLICITY	5. PROMOTIONAL EVENTS	6. ADVERTISING
☐	☐	☐	☐	☐	☐

Where are you stuck or what needs the most work?

☐ Filling the pipeline   ☐ Following up   ☐ Getting presentations   ☐ Closing sales

How much business do you have now? _____

How much business do you *really* want? _____

What would that get you? _____

_____

What is your program goal? _____

What will be your reward? _____

Success Ingredients   Target Date

1. _____   _____

2. _____   _____

3. _____   _____

Daily Actions

1. _____

2. _____

3. _____

4. _____

5. _____

6. _____

7. _____

8. _____

9. _____

10. _____

Special Permission _____

Chapter 3

Where Are You Headed? Setting Your Sales and Marketing Goal

"We can achieve what we can conceive and believe."

—Mark Twain

How Having a Goal Will Help You

In this chapter, you are going to set your sales and marketing goal for the twenty-eight days of the Get Clients Now! program. We will be using goal-setting techniques many times throughout this program, so let's take a moment to examine the system's core philosophy about goals:

1. Set a goal that will stretch you, but that you believe is realistic.

2. Try your best to meet it.

3. When your goal becomes unrealistic, change it.

4. Reward yourself for effort, not just results.

The reward is a key element of the process. Marketing is unpredictable. Sometimes you do everything exactly right and still don't get the results you want when you want them. If you reward yourself only when you get results, all the challenging work that led up to the result often gets discounted. And in the meantime, you feel as though you aren't getting anywhere.

Get into the habit of rewarding yourself for effort, regardless of your results. To do this consistently, you will always need a goal. If you decide, for example, that you will make ten follow-up calls on Monday, and you make them, you deserve some acknowledgment even if none of those people agree to buy today. If you hadn't set a goal for the day, you would have nothing to reward yourself for, and no cushion for the disappointment you may feel.

This approach is particularly important where Success Ingredients are concerned. Having a brochure may be crucial for the success of your business, but the brochure alone will not get you any clients. You will need to call, mail, and so forth before that brochure turns into sales. Therefore, you need to reward yourself up front for all the effort that went into completing the brochure.

Setting marketing goals on a monthly, weekly, and even daily basis can provide you with a number of significant benefits. The first one is an improved focus. Looking at your goals each day will keep them in the forefront of your mind. Knowing that you have only twenty-eight days to achieve the results you want will tighten your focus on marketing and help you to ignore distractions.

Second, your goals will produce evidence. By regularly measuring your level of effort and comparing it to the results you create, you will get a constant reality check on your progress. You will discover right away if you are not working hard enough or are spending precious marketing time on activities like cleaning out your desk drawer. You will also be able to tell when you have done enough and can take a day off without feeling guilty.

Your goals will also provide you with direction. For the next twenty-eight days, you won't need to worry as much about what you should do next to get more clients. Your completed Action Worksheet will indicate exactly what to do. Whenever you feel uncertain about your next move, ask yourself, "Which choice (action, decision, and so forth) is more likely to lead me in the direction of my goals?" Often that reminder is all you will need to stay on the right track.

Finally, your goals can help you with motivation. Post your Action Worksheet on the wall where you will constantly see it. Run a contest with yourself to see how early in the day you can complete your Daily Actions, and then try to beat your own record. Set up a reward for finishing each Success Ingredient project, or reaching a certain percentage mark toward your program goal. Invent a marketing or sales game and make up your own rules. The more fun you can have, the easier the next twenty-eight days will be.

You Gotta Have a Plan

"There are hundreds of ways to market yourself," maintains Rich Fettke, master coach and author of *Extreme Success* (Simon & Schuster, 2002). "You can create a promo kit to send the media, speak at business groups and functions, send out monthly postcards, e-mails, and faxes. You can call people on the phone and personally deliver your unique marketing message.

"You can do any of these things, but will you? You can't do all of them at the same time. The trick to great marketing is to get the same people to hear about you over and over. The only way to do this without being overwhelmed and frustrated is to create a sales and marketing plan and then stick with it. Your plan needs to be specific, measurable, and attainable (with some risk), and include goal dates and deadlines. Setting up daily success habits for yourself will also lead you toward accomplishing your goals, step by step.

"I use the Get Clients Now! system with my own clients to give them an easy-to-follow structure for attracting more business. It gets them into action, and action creates results."

Rich Fettke, MCC
www.fettke.com

What Is a Goal, Anyway?

When you are planning to cook a meal, it's necessary to know if your intended dish is soup or pasta before you begin. To choose the right Success Ingredients and make the best selections from the Action Plan Menu, you must first determine what sort of feast you wish to create. That's where a goal comes in.

A goal is your statement of intention. It is your own personal declaration of what you want, what you plan to focus on, and what you intend to accomplish. Having a sales and marketing goal gives you a destination in your business journey. Only when you know where you are going can you choose the right path to get you there. And you have to be clear about your destination to know when you have arrived.

Many years ago, some unsung champion of goal-setting came up with the acronym SMART to describe the five important characteristics of a meaningful goal:

Specific. Your goal precisely spells out your desired result.

Measurable. The goal states your target in measurable terms so you will know when you have arrived, as well as where you are at any specific moment.

Achievable. A goal is physically possible to accomplish within any defined limitations.

Realistic. Your goal can be accomplished within the specified time and with available resources.

Timed. There is a calendar date by which you plan to achieve your goal.

Here are some examples of SMART goals you might set for the twenty-eight days of the Get Clients Now! program:

Two new clients with signed contracts by the end of the program

Fifteen paying appointments scheduled weekly beginning in Week 2

Twenty-two billable hours worked per week for the full month

Six thousand dollars in business booked for the following month by Week 3

Eight new qualified prospects by the end of the program

Your program goal will help you get into action. If you have a specific target that must be accomplished by a particular date, you will perform tasks that would otherwise languish on a to-do list. It will also help you measure your effectiveness. If you are moving toward your goal, your actions are effective; if you are not moving toward it, they are ineffective, or not effective enough.

Now you're ready to set a goal. As you answer the questions in the next section, write your responses on your Action Worksheet. See the sample worksheet in Figure 3-1 for an example.

Figure 3-1 Beginning to Fill Out the Action Worksheet

GET CLIENTS NOW!™ Action Worksheet

What strategies will you use?

1. DIRECT CONTACT AND FOLLOW-UP	2. NETWORKING AND REFERRAL BUILDING	3. PUBLIC SPEAKING	4. WRITING AND PUBLICITY	5. PROMOTIONAL EVENTS	6. ADVERTISING
☑	☑	☐	☐	☐	☐

Where are you stuck or what needs the most work?

☑ Filling the pipeline   ☐ Following up   ☐ Getting presentations   ☐ Closing sales

How much business do you have now? __11 clients_____

How much business do you *really* want? __20 clients_____

What would that get you? __pay off my credit cards, take a vacation, feel less stressed_____

_____

What is your program goal? __4 new clients by the end of the program_____

What will be your reward? __go on a ski weekend_____

Success Ingredients	Target Date
1. _____	_____
2. _____	_____
3. _____	_____

Daily Actions

1. _____
2. _____
3. _____
4. _____
5. _____
6. _____
7. _____
8. _____
9. _____
10. _____

Special Permission _____

Setting Your Goal for the Program

The place to start in setting your program goal is to look at where you are starting from. *How much business do you have now?* Answer this question in whatever numerical terms you typically use to measure the amount of business you currently have. For example, you could choose (1) the number of clients you have, (2) the quantity of paying appointments scheduled weekly or monthly, (3) the billable hours you have put in or expect, or (4) the dollar amount of business you have booked or already billed.

If you do not already have a way to measure business that works for you, consider what would inform your marketing efforts the most. What number would best tell you whether your marketing is succeeding? Following are some examples:

If you are a(n) . . .	*Your measurement might be . . .*
Account representative	Total number of accounts
Life coach	Total number of ongoing clients
Real estate agent	Total number of listings
Contract trainer	Monthly number of training days scheduled
Image consultant	Monthly number of appointments booked
Psychotherapist	Weekly number of sessions held
Attorney	Billable hours worked monthly
Graphic designer	Billable hours worked weekly
Management consultant	Billable days scheduled monthly
Freelance writer	Dollar amount of assignments booked monthly
Interior designer	Dollar amount invoiced monthly
Financial planner	Dollar amount of assets under management
Salesperson	Dollar volume of sales closed monthly

The important thing to notice about all these measurements is that they are based on numbers you can easily keep updated and track. During the Get Clients Now! program, you will be measuring progress toward your goal each day, so you always must be able to know exactly where you are. If you are an interior designer, for example, it will probably be easier for you to track the dollar amount of your invoices than the net

---

From Dream to Idea to Goal

"In the early phases of a dream, or with a big dream, there may be no evidence that your idea is a good one, or that this is the right time to execute it," counsels Marcia Wieder, author of *Making Your Dreams Come True* (Harmony, 1999) and *Doing Less and Having More* (Quill, 1999). "At that moment, it is essential that you believe in yourself and in your dream. Your belief will be the foundation, a place that you can stand and say, 'I'm going for it because it matters to me and I believe in my dreams.' Then, prove you really do believe in yourself by taking action.

"Make the call, write the letter, map out an action plan, hire a coach, share your dream. Do something and do it now!"

Marcia Wieder
www.dreamcoach.com

---

profit you are earning on each one. Be sure to pick a measurement that you can know on a daily basis.

Now, using the measure you chose, ask yourself *how much business do you really want?* This should be not just what you want by the end of the month, but the pie-in-the-sky, wave-your-magic-wand answer. Don't worry too much about how possible it seems. Allow yourself to think big. Whatever answer you give here is the direction you are headed in.

If you had what you really want—that level of business you just named—*what would that get you?* Would it give you something tangible you have always desired, like enough free time and money to take a two-week tropical cruise? Or is an intangible outcome more important to you, such as peace of mind, or a feeling of success? There's no one correct response here, so choose something that is personally exciting, inspiring, or fulfilling. This answer is your motivation.

Still using the same measure, *what is your program goal* for the month of the Get Clients Now! program? Three new clients? Eighteen paying appointments per week? Twenty billable hours booked weekly? A monthly gross of $5,000? Your goal is what will give you the evidence that your program is working (or not).

Remember the SMART goal-setting characteristics in designing your monthly goal. A program goal must be a measurable target. "More clients" is not a goal; it is a wish. In order for a goal to help you track your progress, it must be numeric because you will be measuring your progress numerically as you move through the program. Your goal should also be a bit of a stretch. Be realistic, but challenge yourself to choose something slightly ambitious.

Finally, if you achieve your goal for the month, *what will be your reward?* Will you buy yourself a present, take some extra time off, have a special dinner? Choose something that will really represent success to you and that you will look forward to having earned at the program's end.

Merely by answering the questions above, you will already be on the path to success. It's part of the magic of goal-setting. When you set a specific goal and begin checking your progress against it on a regular basis, your day-to-day activities start to shift in the direction that supports your goal. This shift begins to happen without any conscious effort on your part. And, of course, additional effort in an informed direction can dramatically enhance the process, as you will see in Chapter 4.

Time for a Reality Check

Setting a realistic goal is important to your success. Choosing a target that is too easy to hit won't stretch you. You need to make an extra effort to produce your best results. But, if you set a goal that is unreasonably high, you will become frustrated and discouraged. So, how do you know if your goal is realistic? Here are four different ways of checking the reality of your goal. Choose whichever one you like best, or use all four:

1. *Straight-Face Test.* One way to use this method is to state your goal out loud, to an audience, in a strong, confident voice. If you can keep a straight face, it's probably realistic. Another way is to ask yourself the question, "Can I really do this?" If the most honest answer you can give yourself is a resounding "Yes!" it is most likely a realistic goal.

2. *Prior Experience.* If the straight-face method seems too simplistic, review your prior experience. Have you ever had a month where you reached the level of success implied by your current goal? If you have, no matter how improbable the set of circumstances was the last time, your goal is still realistic. If you did it before, you can do it again. And remembering that your goal is supposed to be a bit of a stretch, if you even came close to your current goal in some prior month, consider it realistic.

3. *Numerical Analysis.* If you got an inconclusive answer using the first method or are lacking sufficient experience to use the second, try looking at the numbers. Let's say you want to get four new clients this month. How many people do you think you will have to make presentations to in order to get four clients? Eight? Twelve? How many people will you need to make contact with to set up that many presentations? Forty? One hundred twenty? Don't worry if you don't know for sure; just take a guess.

However many you think it is, do you have that many people already in your pipeline, and the time or resources to contact them all? Sit down with your calculator and crunch some numbers. Starting from where you are right now, with the resources you have available, can you deliver the level of effort needed to reach your stated goal in one month?

4. *Peer Comparison.* Have others you would consider peers accomplished a similar goal in their business in one month's time? Do your colleagues or competitors who have been in business about the same length

---

If You Want It, Write It

"Writing down what you want is the basis for all success," declares Sunny Hills, a success coach who publishes weekly affirmations for subscribers in 65 countries from his home on Maui. "So often we focus on saying what we don't want. But if we concentrate on the negative things, that's what we're likely to get. Negative thoughts close doors; positive thoughts open them. If we refocus ourselves on what we do want, we'll get that instead.

"Years ago, when I first read Napoleon Hill's *Think and Grow Rich*, I wrote down what he calls my 'definite chief aim' in life, which included what I hoped to achieve and by when. I thought as big as I could in writing down what I wanted. I never thought I could achieve the things I wrote. Several years later I looked at that piece of paper, and I had achieved everything on it.

"Start visualizing specifically what you want and put it in writing. You can use your written goals as a tuning fork, and tune yourself in to success."

Sunny Hills, CPCC
www.sunnythoughts.com

To Get What You Want, Get Real

"A participant in one of my groups told me that what she got from the Get Clients Now! program was much more valuable than reaching the goal she had set," remembers coach and trainer Ricki Rush, author of *Becoming Your True Self* (Lifeworks, 2005). "She learned to be more compassionate with herself. What she discovered was that she had always set unrealistic goals—too high or too big—which in turn consistently set her up to fail.

"She realized that what she really needed to do was set smaller, more realistic goals. Then she experienced the feeling of winning, which greatly reduced the stress she used to suffer from. By focusing on these smaller steps, she found that she had more energy, and her mental focus was clearer than it had been in a long time."

Ricki Rush, CPCC, CHT
www.lifeworks-coaching.com

---

of time routinely get that much business? If so, you have set a realistic goal, no matter how unattainable it may seem to you right now.

If any of these tests make you fear that the goal you have set is unrealistic, change it now. There's no fun, and even less value, in struggling to meet a goal that was never achievable in the first place.

One final hint: if you are just starting out in business, you might consider setting a goal based on a certain number of leads acquired, prospects contacted, or presentations given rather than closed sales. Remember the length of the marketing cycle for our computer systems consultant in the previous chapter. If you are starting from scratch to fill your pipeline, closing a sale in the next twenty-eight days might be out of reach for you.

Are You Resisting This Process?

Have you read this entire discussion of goal-setting without yet setting a goal? Or did you choose one, but tell yourself, "I don't have to set a real goal. This is just an exercise"? It's time to ask yourself why. Or better yet, what is in the way?

Feel Better to Sell Better

"In numerous conversations with top salespeople over the years, we've found that they all have one thing in common," notes Brian Tracy, author of 30 books on sales and motivation, including *The Psychology of Selling* (Nelson Business, 2005). "They have taken the time to sit down and create a clear blueprint for themselves and their future lives.

"Even if they started the process of goal-setting and personal strategic planning with a little skepticism, they eventually become true believers. Salespeople are amazed by the incredible power of goal setting and strategic planning. Believers often accomplish far more than they ever believed possible in selling and they ascribe their success to the deliberate process of thinking through every aspect of their work and their lives, developing a detailed, written road map, and continually working toward where they want to go.

"Happiness has been defined as 'The progressive achievement of a worthy ideal or goal.' When you work progressively, step-by-step toward something that is important, you generate a continuous feeling of success and achievement. You feel more positive and motivated. You feel more in control of your life, happier, and more fulfilled. Feeling like a winner, you will soon develop the psychological momentum that enables you to overcome obstacles and plough through adversity as you move toward achieving the goals that are most important to you."

Brian Tracy
www.briantracy.com

Are you afraid? Of what? Failing? Succeeding? Offending someone? Looking silly? Do you have some negative past experience with goal-setting that is causing you to avoid it? Whatever it is that is preventing you from choosing a real honest-to-goodness, no-kidding, I-can-do-this goal, get it out in the open now. This program will not work for you unless you set a realistic goal.

Write out your fears and concerns, draw or paint them, talk them out with your business buddy, action group, coach, or a friend. Do whatever it takes to discover what is stopping you, and then stop letting it stop you. Make a conscious choice to try goal-setting one more time, or for the first time. Trust the process. It works.

Locking It In

Great work! Now that you have a goal, find someone to tell it to. If you are working with a buddy, group, or coach, you already have a place to share your goal. If not, tell it to a friend or colleague. Stating goals out loud grants them more reality than just writing them down. And telling someone else what you plan to accomplish creates a sense of accountability on your part to give you an extra push toward that goal.

Part II

The System

Chapter 4

What's Stopping You? Selecting Your Success Ingredients

"Security is mostly a superstition. Life is either a daring adventure or nothing. . . . Avoiding danger is no safer in the long run than outright exposure."

—Helen Keller

What Are the Missing Ingredients?

With a realistic goal in place, you are now ready to take the next step in designing the action plan you will follow for the next month. You will be selecting your Success Ingredients—the missing ingredients you need in order to cook up a successful sales and marketing plan.

Success Ingredients are the tools, information, or skills that will successfully address the area of your marketing you have determined is stuck, or needs more work. Each stage of the Universal Marketing Cycle requires a different list of key ingredients for effective marketing. If you are working on filling the pipeline, for example, you may need to find some new networking events to attend. But if your focus is on closing sales, this ingredient won't be helpful. You might instead need to work on your selling skills.

The place to begin in choosing Success Ingredients is to ask yourself why you are not making progress in your chosen stage of the Universal Marketing Cycle. "Why can't I fill the pipeline?" you might ask. Or, "Why aren't I following up?" Your answer might point you to a needed Success Ingredient right away. Stop and think about this: what tools, information, or skills are you missing to help you fill the pipeline, follow up, get presentations, or close sales?

Shopping for Success Ingredients

In the design of your Get Clients Now! program, you should have at least one, and no more than three, Success Ingredients that you plan to work on over the next month. You may have already thought of some missing ingredients by asking yourself why you are stuck in a particular stage of your marketing. To help you select just the right ingredients for your plan, see the Success Ingredient shopping list in Figure 4-1.

In reviewing the shopping list, it is important that you look at only the section that applies to your chosen marketing stage. Don't overwhelm yourself by checking out all the other options. You have already determined exactly where you need to focus right now, so stay with it. If you are ready to move into another stage later in the month—or the next time you use the program—that will be time enough to look at the other possibilities.

Some of the items on the shopping list may be unfamiliar to you. To help you decide which ingredients are the best for you, see the Success Ingredient Guide in Figure 4-2. There is much more information about these ingredients in the detailed marketing recipes in Part III of this book. However, don't rush to go there right now. You don't need to worry yet about the how-to's of acquiring and employing the ingredients. All you need to do now is choose those you would like to work on first.

Using the "Black-Box" Principle

When an engineer needs to design a new process from scratch, many unknowns can surface—so many, in fact, that if the engineer were to try to answer every necessary question while creating the design, it might become hopelessly bogged down in detail, becoming almost impossible to complete. A handy solution to this obstacle is to enclose each unknown in a black box and design the rest of the process without knowing the details of what goes inside the boxes.

Adopting this idea to design your marketing action plan can be a convenient solution to a common problem experienced by marketers. Let's say you are working on the stage of Filling the Pipeline, and you're pretty sure you will need some "networking venues" in order to start meeting more prospects. Yet you have no idea what those would be or where to find them. Your lack of information might cause you to say, "I can't choose that; I don't know how to go about it," and ignore this important ingredient completely. Or, you might go the other direction and try to fill in the gap in your knowledge by chasing after information about networking in your industry, delaying getting started on your action plan until you have some answers.

By using the black-box principle, you can avoid both of those wrong turns. You can simply choose "networking venues" as something you need, and put it on your Success Ingredient list, without knowing yet how you will acquire it. This is exactly what you should do.

So refer to Part III of this book only if you need additional information to choose one to three ingredients with which you will start. You'll have plenty of opportunities to learn how to accomplish each one once you begin your action plan.

Which Ingredients to Choose

You can choose any of the ingredients listed under your chosen stage of the Universal Marketing Cycle, but you should look most closely at those designated for the marketing strategies you selected in Chapter 2.

Each ingredient shown in the Success Ingredient shopping list in Figure 4-1 displays an icon to the left that indicates for which of the six marketing strategies that ingredient is typically used. (The icons are reviewed for your convenience on page 62.) Some ingredients, such as "business cards" or "website," have all of the icons because they are tools that can be used with any of the strategies. The others are marked with only those icons representing the strategies that each specific ingredient supports.

For example, under the Filling the Pipeline stage you'll see "prospect list" as a Success Ingredient that supports the strategies of (1) direct contact and follow-up, and (2) advertising. This is because you might require a prospect list either for the direct contact strategy of cold calling or the advertising strategy of direct mail.

The best way to use the shopping list is as a source of ideas rather than as a prescription. You may already know exactly what ingredients are missing in your marketing. As you read through the list, keep asking yourself why you can't be or aren't being successful in your stuck area. Place a check mark next to each ingredient you suspect might be missing for you.

The Strategy Icons

  Direct Contact & Follow-Up

 Networking & Referral Building

 Public Speaking

Writing & Publicity

 Promotional Events

 **Advertising**

Editing Your Shopping List

If you chose three Success Ingredients or fewer, you can skip to the next section, "Setting Target Completion Dates." If you selected more than three, it's time to prioritize. To ensure you are choosing the most important ingredients, first look at the marketing strategies you have decided to use. Since you will be using only those strategies for the present, you can eliminate any ingredients that you don't actually need to implement your chosen strategies.

For example, if you are working on filling the pipeline, but did not choose writing and publicity as one of your strategies, you should not be selecting "publicity venues" or "blog concept/topics" as Success Ingredients, no matter how attractive they sound. You have spent quite a bit of effort already in diagnosing the area that needs more work and picking the right strategies to address it, so don't second-guess yourself now.

(text continues page 69)

Figure 4-1 Success Ingredient Shopping List

To fill the pipeline...

- Description of services
- Market niche definition
- 10-second introduction
- Business cards
- Website
- Prospect list
- Lead sources
- Networking venues
- Referral partners
- Networking skills
- Web promotion strategy
- Speaking venues
- Speaking topics/bio
- Writing venues
- Article or query letter
- Publicity venues
- Press release/media kit
- Blog concept/topics
- Promotion concept
- Promotion plan
- Advertising venues
- Flyer venues
- Ad copy, layout, or script

(continues)

Figure 4-1 Success Ingredient Shopping List (*continued*)

To follow up more effectively...

- Brochure
- Marketing kit
- Model marketing letter
- Contact management system
- 30-second commercial
- In-house mailing list
- Postcard or mailer
- Newsletter or e-zine
- E-mail autoresponders
- Personal connections

To turn more contacts into presentations...

- Telemarketing script/skills
- Qualifying questions
- Higher-quality leads and referrals
- Stickier website
- Professional visibility
- Competitive research
- Target market research
- New market position
- Better service package
- Narrower focus of services

To turn more presentations into sales...

- Better-qualified prospects
- Stronger relationships
- Presentation script/visuals
- Presentation skills
- Selling script
- Selling skills
- Portfolio
- Leave-behind
- Professional credibility
- Testimonials or references

Figure 4-2 Success Ingredient Guide

Filling the Pipeline

- *Description of Services*. A clear, specific oral and written description of the features, benefits, structure, and cost of your services.

- *Market Niche Definition*. Description of the target market you most wish to do business with and the area in which you specialize.

- *10-Second Introduction*. Self-introduction that describes what you do and who you do it for in a clear and memorable way.

- *Business Cards*. An effective card specifically states what you do, but doesn't contain a laundry list of your talents. Don't list multiple businesses on the same card.

- *Website*. A basic site tells visitors what you do and why they should hire you. More powerful is a site that allows prospects to sample your expertise, provides free tools or resources, and captures visitors' contact information for future interaction.

- *Prospect List*. List of people or companies unknown to you, but that fit your market niche definition. You acquire a list like this through purchase, exchange, or research.

- *Lead Sources*. Groups, events, institutions, publications, websites, and broadcast media that can give you information about potential clients on a regular basis.

- *Networking Venues*. Places, groups, events, and online communities where you can meet prospective clients and referral partners.

- *Referral Partners*. People, groups, or institutions that are willing to refer potential clients to you on a regular basis.

- *Networking Skills*. Techniques or experience you need to feel more comfortable about networking. You might read a book, take a workshop, or practice with friends.

- *Web Promotion Strategy*. Plan for increasing the visibility of your website. Techniques might include search engine optimization, adding keyword-rich content, publishing articles online, requesting links from other websites, or paid advertising.

- *Speaking Venues*. Places, groups, or events where you might be able to speak to promote your business.

- *Speaking Topics/Bio*. Description of one to three topics you are available to speak on, plus a summary of your background and experience. You send this to potential speaking venues to pique their interest.

(continues)

Figure 4-2 (*continued*)

- *Writing Venues*. Publications or websites for which you can write articles, tips, or an ongoing column.

- *Article or Query Letter*. Completed article, tip, or inquiry you send to potential writing venues. Some venues want to see finished articles; others prefer that you send a query letter before writing.

- *Publicity Venues*. Print, broadcast, and online media outlets you can approach to get quoted, interviewed, or profiled.

- *Press Release/Media Kit*. A release is a bulletin you send to the media to attract press coverage. Following up may require a media kit including your bio or company profile, photo, examples of other press coverage, or sample interview questions.

- *Blog Concept/Topics*. A blog is a website to which you post regular updates in a journal format. Like articles, a blog can attract new prospects while building credibility.

- *Promotion Concept*. Idea for a promotional event, such as a free demonstration or workshop, or an exhibit at a trade show.

- *Promotion Plan*. Your plan for producing a promotional event or trade show appearance.

- *Advertising Venues*. Media you can advertise in to reach your market niche: direct mail, newspapers, magazines, newsletters, trade journals, directories, websites, search engines, e-zines, broadcast e-mail, radio, or TV.

- *Flyer Venues*. Places where you can post, distribute, or circulate a flyer.

- *Ad Copy, Layout, or Script*. What your proposed ad will say and how it will look.

Following Up

- *Brochure*. May be simple and inexpensive or deluxe and very pricey. Think of it primarily as a follow-up tool, rather than for filling the pipeline.

- *Marketing Kit*. Often replaces a brochure, especially in business-to-business marketing. Includes several pieces (e.g., description of services, professional bio, client list, testimonials, or articles).

- *Model Marketing Letter*. Boilerplate you pick and choose from to create letters you send to contacts, rather than writing each one from scratch. Can often replace a brochure.

- *Contact Management System.* Method of keeping track of all your contacts. Could be 3 × 5-inch cards, a notebook, a handheld device like a Palm, Pocket PC, or smartphone, or desktop computer software such as ACT! or Outlook.

- *30-Second Commercial.* Brief verbal summary of what you do and who you do it for. Useful for opening presentations, leaving voice mail messages, and at networking and leads groups.

- *In-House Mailing List.* List of clients, prospects, and referral partners who already know you. These are names you have accumulated from prior contacts, networking, referrals, speaking, promotional events, etc.

- *Postcard or Mailer.* A piece of literature you send by postal mail to your mailing list to remind prospects that you are still around, or make a special offer.

- *Newsletter or E-Zine.* Allows you to demonstrate your expertise and follow up at the same time. Can be a print version sent by postal mail or an e-mail version.

- *E-Mail Autoresponders.* Automated e-mails sent to prospects who inquire about your services via e-mail or on your website. Can be programmed in a series to follow up over time.

- *Personal Connections.* If following up is challenging because your prospects all feel like strangers, you may need stronger personal connections. This can include referrals, introductions, more research, attending events, volunteering, and more.

Getting Presentations

- *Telemarketing Script/Skills.* The language and techniques to help you improve at selling yourself by phone. Might include better opening questions, answers to common objections, or practice at asking for an opportunity to present.

- *Qualifying Questions.* Questions you ask up front to determine whether someone is a good prospect for your service. Only qualified prospects are worth your time and effort to follow up with.

- *Higher Quality Leads and Referrals.* The type of prospects who are most likely to buy, based on their profile or the source of the original lead. Developing a profile of your best potential clients will help you seek out more leads that fit that profile.

- *Stickier Website.* Features added to your website that encourage visitors to stay longer, explore more, and give you their contact informa-

(continues)

Figure 4-2 (*continued*)

tion for follow-up. Can include articles, online assessments or other tools, useful resources, and more.

• *Professional Visibility*. Making yourself more visible in your market niche will increase the likelihood that prospects know your name before you contact them. Might include speaking, writing, publicity, volunteering, and other tactics.

• *Competitive Research*. Information about the competition that enables you to better compete. When you know what clients like about competitors, you can emulate it; when you know what clients dislike, you can show them how you are better.

• *Target Market Research*. Information about your prospective clients that tells you more about what they want and need. May take the form of a questionnaire, survey, focus group, or research in trade or consumer literature.

• *New Market Position*. Your market position is how prospects think of you in comparison to your competitors. You can change your position by crafting a different marketing message to sell your services verbally, in writing, on the Web, etc.

• *Better Service Package*. A different way of packaging your services to make them more attractive to prospective clients. It might entail changing how you set or charge fees, bundling different services together, or including products in your package.

• *Narrower Focus of Services*. Limiting what you present to the one or two lines of business that your prospects are most likely to buy. A narrower focus will allow prospects to better grasp what you have to offer.

Closing Sales

• *Better Qualified Prospects*. If your presentations aren't turning into sales, this may be the first place to look. Refer to "Qualifying questions" and "Higher-quality leads and referrals" above. You may need either or both to find better prospects to present to.

• *Stronger Relationships*. You may be trying to close sales too soon, before prospects have learned to trust you. A longer relationship-building period may be needed, using tactics like lunch or coffee, invitations to events, and sending articles or a newsletter.

• *Presentation Script/Visuals*. An outline of what you plan to present and supporting visuals to make your services more tangible. Includes questions you need to ask and responses to questions you might get.

- *Presentation Skills*. Techniques or experience you need to get more comfortable with questioning, listening, or presenting. You might take a workshop, listen to an audio, work with a coach, or join a group to practice.

- *Selling Script*. A list of important points to remember when selling. Your script should include asking-for-the-business questions, and answers to common objections.

- *Selling Skills*. Techniques or experience you need to do a better job at closing the sale. Books, workshops, and role play with a colleague or coach can all be helpful.

- *Portfolio*. Tangible examples of your work that you can show to a prospect. Case studies, photographs, and samples of designs, writing, or reports can all help to make a sale.

- *Leave-Behind*. Something extra you leave with, or send to, a prospect to look over after your presentation. It reminds the client of you and gives you another reason to follow up soon.

- *Professional Credibility*. Increasing your credibility will cut down on questions about your background and experience. You may need to emphasize your existing credentials more, or work on acquiring better credentials to present.

- *Testimonials or References*. Letters or quotes from satisfied clients, or a list of impressive references, with their contact information. Can be provided in a letter, brochure, marketing kit, e-zine, or on your website.

If you eliminate those distractions and still have more than three Success Ingredients, ask yourself which three you need first. During your Get Clients Now! program month, you will be acquiring or creating the one to three ingredients you choose. As you complete your first choices, you can cross them off the list and start work on others.

Let's say you are focusing on following up, and are considering the Success Ingredients "model marketing letter," "contact management system," "30-second commercial," and "e-zine." It would make more sense to begin with the first three, since the model marketing letter, contact management system, and 30-second commercial would all help you follow up with hot prospects you already know are interested, while the e-zine would be more helpful with contacts you know less about or with whom you need to build more trust first. If you complete any one of the three within the month, you could then start work on the e-zine.

Bridging the Gap from Idea to Action

"Often what happens is people get very excited about their dreams, passions, and visions," describe Leslie Lupinsky and Joni Mar, authors of *The Inspired Business Approach* (Design for Living, 2005), "but when it comes to the implementation phase, they fall into despair or fear about the work involved to achieve the results they are after. Once this starts, it can be a downward cycle. The person procrastinates on the necessary actions, producing more fear and despair. It takes a great deal of courage and support as well as a strong commitment to turn the cycle around.

"If you are losing momentum in your business, try asking yourself these questions:

1. Where are you now?
2. Where do you want to be?
3. What feelings are you experiencing in this gap between the two?
4. What's the cost to you and your business of staying here?
5. Sit with the experience of the gap, your feelings, and all of their implications for several minutes.
6. Now, where are you willing to move forward into action? What would support you to take the next step?"

Leslie Lupinsky, MCC, CPCC
www.leslielupinsky.com
Joni Mar, PCC, CPCC
www.jonimar.com

The Success Ingredients you choose don't necessarily need to be completed within one month; you are just deciding to work on them during that time. A 30-second commercial is something you might knock off in a couple of hours, but building a website might take you six weeks from start to finish.

If you're still not sure which ingredients you should choose, skip to Part III, which has a chapter for each stage of the Universal Marketing Cycle. See what the chapter for your chosen stage has to say about the Success Ingredients you are considering, and then pick no more than three to start with.

Setting Target Completion Dates

It's time to record those Success Ingredients on your Action Worksheet. Look at the example in Figure 4-3. List the ingredients you have chosen on the Success Ingredients section of your own worksheet; notice that the example shows target dates for each one. You need to do this, too, so think about what would be a realistic amount of time to allow yourself to complete or acquire each item. It's okay to choose a target date that is more than a month away.

In setting a target date for your Success Ingredients, use the guidelines introduced in Chapter 3 for realistic goal-setting. Review the "Time for a Reality Check" section if you need a refresher. You should consider both the actual time and the elapsed time needed for completion.

If you decided you were finally going to finish that brochure you've been working on, it might only take you two hours to complete a final review of the last draft your graphic designer sent you. But then it will take the designer time to make your changes and get it to the printer, and the printer will need time to get it on the press. So estimate how much elapsed time will be required to get it all done.

If you aren't sure, don't leave the target date blank while you check with the designer and the printer to see what is reasonable. Allowing others to determine your schedule may be one of the habits that has gotten you into trouble in the past. Try this instead: decide when you would like to have the printed brochure in your hand; then call the designer and say, "I need to have my brochure complete by the 31st. If I get you my final changes by the 20th, can you meet that date?" If your request is unreasonable, the designer will tell you. Then you can negotiate for a new date, and change the target date on your worksheet.

The function of having a target date for each Success Ingredient, just like setting a marketing goal, is to get you into action immediately. Once your brochure has a due date, you will make a call about it and say, "This is when I need it," instead of, "When can you have it?" You will immediately be in more control of your marketing, and much more likely to produce results sooner.

Changing the target date after establishing it is not cheating; it is being realistic. What is the point of beating yourself up because you failed to meet a target date that you had already discovered was impossible? It's much better to keep your target dates realistic so you can reward yourself for reaching them. This goal-setting technique is particularly important regarding Success Ingredients. Having a great brochure may be important to the success of your business, but the

Figure 4-3 Adding Success Ingredients to the Action Worksheet

GET CLIENTS NOW!™ Action Worksheet

What strategies will you use?

1. DIRECT CONTACT AND FOLLOW-UP	2. NETWORKING AND REFERRAL BUILDING	3. PUBLIC SPEAKING	4. WRITING AND PUBLICITY	5. PROMOTIONAL EVENTS	6. ADVERTISING
☑	☑	☐	☐	☐	☐

Where are you stuck or what needs the most work?

☑ Filling the pipeline ☐ Following up ☐ Getting presentations ☐ Closing sales

How much business do you have now? __11 clients__

How much business do you *really* want? __20 clients__

What would that get you? __pay off my credit cards, take a vacation, feel less stressed__

What is your program goal? __4 new clients by the end of the program__

What will be your reward? __go on a ski weekend__

Success Ingredients	Target Date
1. __market niche definition__	10/06/06
2. __10-second introduction__	10/13/06
3. __3 networking venues__	10/20/06

Daily Actions

1. _____
2. _____
3. _____
4. _____
5. _____
6. _____
7. _____
8. _____
9. _____
10. _____

Special Permission _____

Make Your Projects Bite-Size

"Finding space in your busy life for a big project like developing a website can be a challenge," points out Caterina Rando, speaker, success coach, and author of *Learn to Power Think* (Chronicle, 2002). "Sometimes we have so much to do that we feel paralyzed. When that happens, write down everything you think you need to do. Decide what is urgent, and what you can put off. Ask yourself if there is anything you can forget about doing, and if there's anything that someone else can do.

"Try working in increments. Tell yourself you will give yourself a break in an hour. Psychologically, you will feel more at ease with the situation. At the end of the hour, take a break, even if it is just a walk down the hall. This is also good for the creative process; it gives your conscious mind an opportunity to wander and come up with some new ideas.

"If you are really dreading doing something, find a way to make it fun. I always pay my bills while watching a *Star Trek* rerun; that makes it tolerable. I have a client who returns all possible phone calls from her Jacuzzi early in the morning. Play upbeat music when working in your office.

"Break down your project into bite-size chunks. I used to tell myself that I would take a whole day and do nothing else but clean my office. I never did it because the idea was too dreadful. Instead, what I do now is work on it in 15-minute segments.

"I often procrastinate when I need to do some writing. The mental block that is in my way is that I believe or feel that I don't know how to say what I want to say. But if I sit down and start tapping on the keyboard, it will work itself out. So don't sit around wondering how you might get it done, simply start to do it and see what happens."

Caterina Rando, MCC
www.caterinar.com

brochure alone will not get you any clients. You will need to call, mail, follow up, and so forth before that brochure helps you land a presentation, and ultimately, a client. Therefore, you need to reward yourself up front for all the effort that went into completing the brochure before waiting to see the results it helps you produce.

Climbing the Marketing Ladder

Grace Durfee is a personal coach who uses the Get Clients Now! system as one of her tools to help clients succeed. According to Grace, "Success Ingredients in marketing are like the ladders in the classic children's game *Chutes and Ladders*. Your good efforts catapult you from one level of play to another, putting you closer to your goal. But it's not a lucky spin of the wheel that lands you on a ladder space and helps you get ahead. In marketing, intention, planning, and consistent action are what propel you forward. Careful selection of Success Ingredients is an important part of your marketing plan. You want to choose projects that have lasting impact—that get you out of a stuck place in your marketing, once and for all.

"How do you determine what the best Success Ingredients are for you at this time? A key question to ask is, 'What would make the biggest difference?' If you're not sure, your excuses provide clues that will point you in the right direction. Examine the excuses you make over and over again. For instance, if you say, 'I'm not good at networking because I get tongue-tied when people ask what I do,' then working on a 10-second introduction would be a wise choice for a Success Ingredient. 'I couldn't follow up with that prospect because I lost his business card,' could mean that it's time to transfer your fish bowl full of business cards into a contact management system. Perhaps you say, 'I'm uncomfortable putting myself out there as a professional, because I don't have _____ yet.' Fill in the blank here with your missing link, whether it's a business card, marketing materials, or a website. You've just found your Success Ingredient project.

"Completing a Success Ingredient will give you a burst of energy, confidence, and ideas for the next project. No chutes for you, you're finding the next ladder!"

Grace Durfee
www.balancewithgrace.com

Quantifying Your Success Ingredients

When setting target completion dates for your Success Ingredients, you may be puzzled about what to do if your Success Ingredient is a skill set instead of something tangible. Let's say that you want to improve your networking skills. Pick a target date by which you would like to have this ingredient completed and imagine that you are scoring yourself on a scale of zero to 100 percent. If zero percent means you can't network at all, and 100 percent means you are a star networker, what would be your score today? Perhaps twenty-five or fifty percent? Now what would you like your score to be by the target date you chose? That's the answer you would write on your worksheet. For example, you might write "networking skills at 75%—Oct. 27."

You can use this same scoring technique to set targets for other intangible Success Ingredients, like "professional credibility" or "better service package." Just pick your desired completion date and decide the score you would like to achieve by then. If this seems arbitrary, it is. Yet you are the only one who can accurately measure your own progress. The goal and your progress toward it have to make sense and feel good to you. That's the only way a goal can work its motivation magic.

Even tangible Success Ingredients might require some quantification in order to be specific enough to serve as a goal. If you chose "writing venues," for example, how many are enough? Pick a number that would make you feel as if you had satisfied that need for at least a month's time, and write it on your worksheet—for example, "10 writing venues."

Once you have chosen one to three Success Ingredients, written them on your Action Worksheet, assigned target dates to them, and quantified them in terms of number needed or scores you wish to achieve, you have completed four of the six steps in designing your Get Clients Now! program. In Chapter 5 you will be choosing the precise action steps you will take to get clients over the next twenty-eight days.

Here's What to Do: Choosing from the Action Plan Menu

"We must not sit down and wait for miracles. Up, and be going!"
—John Eliot, seventeenth-century British missionary

Where Do the Clients Come From?

The final, and most important, piece of designing your own personal Get Clients Now! program is to select the specific marketing and sales action steps you plan to take on a regular basis over the next month. These are the actions that will generate business for you.

At the beginning of this book, you learned the most important secret of professional services marketing and sales: The magic formula is choosing a set of simple, effective things to do, and doing them consistently. That's where the clients come from.

You are about to do exactly this. You are going to choose ten specific actions to take, and perform them daily or weekly for the next twenty-eight days. What you choose will be based on the "stuck" place you uncovered with the Universal Marketing Cycle, as well as the marketing strategies you selected to address that area in need of more work. These action steps are designed to enable you to dramatically improve your marketing. But you need to actually do them in order to find clients.

There is an interesting phenomenon that occurs when you get serious about marketing in a focused, consistent way. You begin to get results in unexpected places. The telephone rings, and it's a prospect you spoke to three months ago saying he is suddenly interested in working with you. You go to a networking meeting that seems like a complete waste of time while you are there, and run into a hot new prospect in the elevator on your way out. You get an exciting referral from someone whose name you don't even recognize. It's almost as if the universe has noticed how hard you are working and decided to reward you.

Don't make the mistake of thinking that these out-of-the-blue opportunities are accidents. There is a direct connection between the level of effort you put into marketing and the results you get out of it, even when it seems as if the results are completely unrelated to your efforts.

This phenomenon is so common with people who use the Get Clients Now! program that it has a name: the Persistence Effect. If you persist in making ten calls a day, every day, you will get business, but it won't all come from the calls you made. If you consistently attend one networking event per week, clients will appear, but not necessarily from the events you attended. Don't worry about why it works; just know that it works.

The existence of the Persistence Effect can help you enormously in

---

Build a Fire Under It

"Persistence is an essential factor in the procedure of transmuting desire into its monetary equivalent," wrote Napoleon Hill in his classic *Think and Grow Rich* (1938). "The basis of persistence is the power of will . . .

"The majority of people are ready to throw their aims and purposes overboard, and give up at the first sign of opposition or misfortune. A few carry on despite all opposition, until they attain their goal . . .

"Lack of persistence is one of the major causes of failure. Moreover, experience with thousands of people has proved that lack of persistence is a weakness common to the majority of men. It is a weakness which may be overcome by effort. The ease with which lack of persistence may be conquered will depend entirely on the intensity of one's desire.

"The starting point of all achievement is desire. Keep this constantly in mind. Weak desires bring weak results, just as a small amount of fire makes a small amount of heat. If you find yourself lacking in persistence, this weakness may be remedied by building a stronger fire under your desires."

Napoleon Hill
1883–1970

choosing the Daily Actions for your program, because there is one more secret to successful marketing: it doesn't matter so much what you choose as it does *that* you choose.

Picking ten things you can do about marketing—and actually doing them—will break you out of analysis paralysis, give you a plan, and get you into action. Even if you picked the "wrong" ten actions, the Persistence Effect would make this focused activity pay off for you in some way. Would it pay off as well as picking the "right" ten things? Probably not. That's why you are about to choose only actions that represent the stage of the marketing cycle you are focusing on and the marketing strategies you already selected.

Ordering from the Action Plan Menu

There are two ways of going about selecting what Daily Actions to include in your program. One way is to choose from the selections already prepared for you that appear on the Action Plan Menu (Figure 5-1). The other is to design your own unique actions. Let's look first at how to design your own.

Suppose you are focusing on closing sales, and you have chosen direct contact and follow-up as one of your marketing strategies. How could you use this strategy to close more sales? Perhaps you could follow up better by recontacting people who you have already presented to, but didn't buy from you at the time. To turn this into a specific, consistent action, give it a time frame and quantify it—for example, "Follow up with five prospects each week who previously said no."

How do you know how often to do something and how much of it to do? You guess. How much activity do you think will be necessary to achieve the result you want? How much do you have time for? The right answer is probably somewhere between those two. But really, there is no right answer. It doesn't matter so much what you choose as it does *that* you choose.

Remember the Get Clients Now! goal-setting philosophy:

1. Set a goal that will stretch you but that you believe is realistic.

2. Try your best to meet it.

3. When your goal becomes unrealistic, change it.

4. Reward yourself for effort, not just results.

You're going to use these same principles again in designing your Daily Actions. Pick a time frame and quantity that seem reasonable. Try it out. If it's not working, change it. And reward yourself for what you did, not what you got.

You can choose to perform an action daily, weekly, or several times per week. "Daily" typically means five days per week, which is the recommended schedule for the Get Clients Now! program. The only rule is that all actions must be performed at least weekly, because you need to develop consistency in your marketing in order for the Persistence Effect to work. While it's okay to change the frequency of your actions once you start the program, it's generally not a good idea to change the actions themselves until you are ready to move forward to the next stage of the Universal Marketing Cycle.

Now that you know how the process of designing a Daily Action works, take a look at the Action Plan Menu in Figure 5-1. The menu is divided into three sections:

Appetizers—actions that will help you to create or acquire Success Ingredients

Main Course—actions focused directly on getting business

Dessert—actions to help you be more effective and productive in general

You are going to choose ten Daily Actions, either from the menu, or of your own design. As with a meal, you will need to balance your selections. The best combination for a satisfying marketing banquet is one or two actions from the Appetizer menu, seven or eight entrees from the Main Course section, and one Dessert. This design will create an effective balance between project work (e.g., building a website), actual business development (e.g., making cold calls), and self-management (e.g., getting enough sleep) in your action plan.

Start with the Fun Stuff

In a few pages, you will be choosing your Main Course selections, those actions that will directly get you business. It's a good bet that the process of making those choices may bring up some fear and resistance for you, so let's start with the fun stuff: Appetizers and Dessert.

Appetizers are action items to move you forward in the process of cre-

(*text continues page 83*)

Figure 5-1 Action Plan Menu

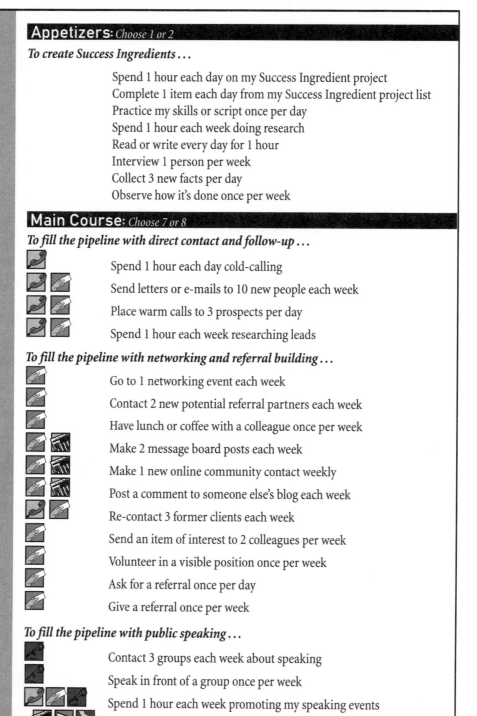

Appetizers: *Choose 1 or 2*

To create Success Ingredients . . .

Spend 1 hour each day on my Success Ingredient project
Complete 1 item each day from my Success Ingredient project list
Practice my skills or script once per day
Spend 1 hour each week doing research
Read or write every day for 1 hour
Interview 1 person per week
Collect 3 new facts per day
Observe how it's done once per week

Main Course: *Choose 7 or 8*

To fill the pipeline with direct contact and follow-up . . .

Spend 1 hour each day cold-calling

Send letters or e-mails to 10 new people each week

Place warm calls to 3 prospects per day

Spend 1 hour each week researching leads

To fill the pipeline with networking and referral building . . .

Go to 1 networking event each week

Contact 2 new potential referral partners each week

Have lunch or coffee with a colleague once per week

Make 2 message board posts each week

Make 1 new online community contact weekly

Post a comment to someone else's blog each week

Re-contact 3 former clients each week

Send an item of interest to 2 colleagues per week

Volunteer in a visible position once per week

Ask for a referral once per day

Give a referral once per week

To fill the pipeline with public speaking . . .

Contact 3 groups each week about speaking

Speak in front of a group once per week

Spend 1 hour each week promoting my speaking events

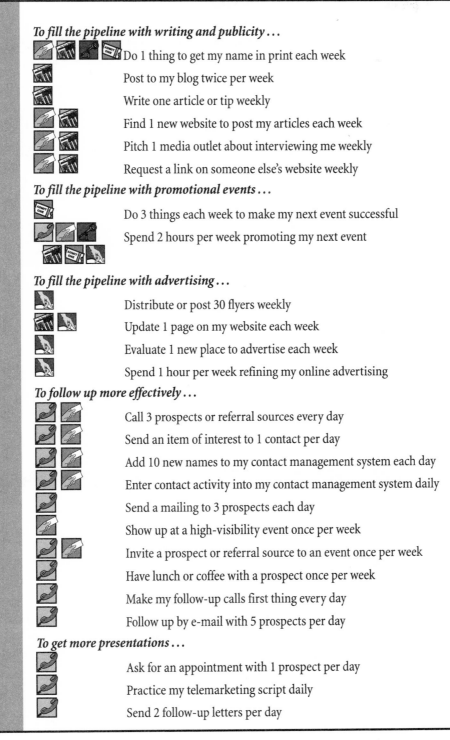

To fill the pipeline with writing and publicity . . .

Do 1 thing to get my name in print each week

Post to my blog twice per week

Write one article or tip weekly

Find 1 new website to post my articles each week

Pitch 1 media outlet about interviewing me weekly

Request a link on someone else's website weekly

To fill the pipeline with promotional events . . .

Do 3 things each week to make my next event successful

Spend 2 hours per week promoting my next event

To fill the pipeline with advertising . . .

Distribute or post 30 flyers weekly

Update 1 page on my website each week

Evaluate 1 new place to advertise each week

Spend 1 hour per week refining my online advertising

To follow up more effectively . . .

Call 3 prospects or referral sources every day

Send an item of interest to 1 contact per day

Add 10 new names to my contact management system each day

Enter contact activity into my contact management system daily

Send a mailing to 3 prospects each day

Show up at a high-visibility event once per week

Invite a prospect or referral source to an event once per week

Have lunch or coffee with a prospect once per week

Make my follow-up calls first thing every day

Follow up by e-mail with 5 prospects per day

To get more presentations . . .

Ask for an appointment with 1 prospect per day

Practice my telemarketing script daily

Send 2 follow-up letters per day

(continues)

Figure 5-1 Action Plan Menu (*continued*)

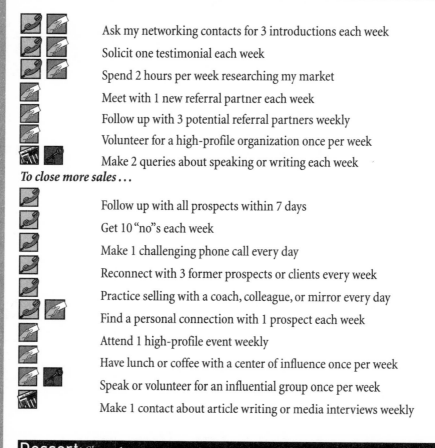

Ask my networking contacts for 3 introductions each week

Solicit one testimonial each week

Spend 2 hours per week researching my market

Meet with 1 new referral partner each week

Follow up with 3 potential referral partners weekly

Volunteer for a high-profile organization once per week

Make 2 queries about speaking or writing each week

To close more sales . . .

Follow up with all prospects within 7 days

Get 10 "no"s each week

Make 1 challenging phone call every day

Reconnect with 3 former prospects or clients every week

Practice selling with a coach, colleague, or mirror every day

Find a personal connection with 1 prospect each week

Attend 1 high-profile event weekly

Have lunch or coffee with a center of influence once per week

Speak or volunteer for an influential group once per week

Make 1 contact about article writing or media interviews weekly

Dessert: *Choose 1*

To be more effective in everything I do . . .

Plan my day each morning

Do all my "A-list" tasks first each day

Write in my success journal each evening

Exercise 3 times per week

Get 8 hours of sleep every night

Meditate for 1/2 hour per day

Schedule a day of fun each week

Add up my income and expenses each week

Spend 1/2 hour each day organizing my office

Visualize success daily

ating or acquiring your chosen Success Ingredients. By putting one or two Appetizers on your list of Daily Actions, you are making a commitment to do what it takes to get those missing ingredients in place. If you chose only one Success Ingredient, you probably only need one Appetizer, but with two or three ingredients to create, you may want two Appetizers to help you along.

The Appetizers on the Action Plan Menu are suggested actions for you to choose from, but you can also design your own. Remember that the time frame and quantity are up to you in either case. Here are some ways you can use the Appetizers on the menu:

- *Spend 1 hour each day on my Success Ingredient project.* Good for projects like "lead sources" or "publicity venues" that may take a while to ferret out.

- *Complete 1 item each day from my Success Ingredient project list.* Use this for projects such as "website" or "contact management system" where you may have a list of many steps to complete.

- *Practice my skills or script once per day.* An excellent choice for ingredients like "telemarketing script/skills," where you need to practice to make progress.

- *Spend 1 hour each week doing research.* Appropriate for ingredients such as "speaking venues" or "competitive research."

- *Read or write every day for 1 hour.* Use this for information-gathering projects like finding "advertising venues," or creative work such as writing an "article or query letter."

- *Interview 1 person per week.* Good for projects such as researching your "market niche definition" or discovering how to find "better-qualified prospects."

- *Collect 3 new facts per day.* Another useful method of quantifying your progress in research or information-gathering.

- *Observe how it's done once per week.* A great way to improve your skills in areas like networking or selling.

When you have chosen one or two Appetizers, write them down as the first two Daily Actions on your Action Worksheet. See Figure 5-2 for an example.

Next, look at the *Dessert* selections. The Daily Actions on the Dessert menu are suggested ways in which you can be more effective and productive in everything you do. Choose just one. To make the right choice,

Figure 5-2 Adding Daily Actions to the Action Worksheet

GET CLIENTS NOW!™ Action Worksheet

What strategies will you use?

1. DIRECT CONTACT AND FOLLOW-UP	2. NETWORKING AND REFERRAL BUILDING	3. PUBLIC SPEAKING	4. WRITING AND PUBLICITY	5. PROMOTIONAL EVENTS	6. ADVERTISING
☑	☑	☐	☐	☐	☐

Where are you stuck or what needs the most work?

☑ Filling the pipeline   ☐ Following up   ☐ Getting presentations   ☐ Closing sales

How much business do you have now? __11 clients__

How much business do you *really* want? __20 clients__

What would that get you? __pay off my credit cards, take a vacation, feel less stressed__

What is your program goal? __4 new clients by the end of the program__

What will be your reward? __go on a ski weekend__

Success Ingredients	Target Date
1. market niche definition	10/06/06
2. 10-second introduction	10/13/06
3. 3 networking venues	10/20/06

Daily Actions

1. Spend 1/2 hour each day on my Success Ingredient project
2. Send letters or e-mails to 6 new people each week
3. Place warm calls to 2 prospects per day
4. Go to 1 networking event each week
5. Contact 3 new potential referral partners each week
6. Have lunch or coffee with a colleague once per week
7. Make 3 message board posts each week
8. Send an item of interest to 3 colleagues per week
9. Ask for a referral once per day
10. Visualize success daily

Special Permission __I give myself permission to have enough time for everything__

It's Okay to Be Yourself

"Many times, the first draft of a marketing action plan reflects all the false conceptions of what a person thinks they need to do in order to succeed at marketing," relates veteran Get Clients Now! facilitator Joan Friedlander. "I love that moment when people figure this out and start coming up with plans that reflect who they are, and what they really like to do. They're much more successful, and happier too.

"There are probably 100 different marketing tactics that you could choose from. You are not going to be excellent at executing all of them. Do yourself a huge favor and choose only those action items that you can actually see yourself doing.

"Are you most comfortable connecting with prospects one-on-one? Go to meetings and events where you are likely to meet prospects or referral partners. Then, rather than trying to land a client in that noisy environment, invite people you want to get to know better to have coffee with you instead.

"Do you hate cold calling? Don't put it on your plan. Instead, build your Daily Actions around warm calling and referral building. A client I worked with made this one simple change and completely altered his results—as well as his feelings—about marketing.

"The only thing you're required to become good at is talking to people so they can understand what you offer and that you can help them. This takes just two things from you: time and practice. It's okay to start right where you are."

Joan Friedlander
www.lifeworkpartners.com

---

ask yourself what is likely to get in the way of your success this month. Have you identified any habits or behaviors that tend to sabotage you? Is there something you need to do for yourself to perform at your best?

Use these descriptions of the Dessert selections on the Action Plan Menu to help you choose one or design your own:

- *Plan my day each morning.* If you often come to the end of the day and wonder where it went, this Dessert may be a good choice for you. Planning your day in advance will take only five or ten minutes. You could also make your plan the night before.

- *Do all my "A-list" tasks first each day.* Not everything on your personal to-do list is of equal value. Try giving every item on the list a priority of A, B, or C, then take care of all the A-items first each day.

- *Write in my success journal each evening.* It's easy to get caught up in failures and shortcomings, but every day has successes in it. Start a success journal, where you write each day only those things you enjoyed, felt good about accomplishing, or for which you received recognition.

- *Exercise 3 times per week.* If you find that regular exercise gives you more energy, it may be just as important to effective marketing as a good telephone script.

- *Get 8 hours of sleep every night.* Depriving yourself of sleep is not good time management, and will backfire quickly. Not everyone needs eight hours, so substitute the best number for your needs.

- *Meditate for 1/2 hour per day.* Meditation, drawing or painting, listening to music, gardening, and needlework are just a few of the many activities that allow for relaxation and quiet reflection. Just plain wool gathering is fine, too. The idea is to give your overworked brain a rest.

- *Schedule a day of fun each week.* Relaxation takes many forms and you may need some pleasurable activity more than a rest. Scheduling fun time in advance will ensure it happens.

- *Add up my income and expenses each week.* Think of this as a motivational technique. If you know you need to make another $500 this week, you may want to pick up the phone on Friday afternoon. If you see your hard work paying off, you may be inspired to do a little more.

- *Spend 1/2 hour each day organizing my office.* Keeping track of where each prospect is in the marketing cycle can be crucial to closing sales. Time spent looking for important information that has gone missing is time you don't have available for marketing.

- *Visualize success daily.* This is a proven technique for improved achievement. Spend a few minutes each day visualizing yourself succeeding at marketing, selling, and earning the rewards that are important to you. You may even want to do this three times a day.

After reading these descriptions, you may be tempted to choose more than one Dessert. Yet you do need to leave enough room for the Main

Course, so limit yourself to just one. If one of the Desserts on the menu caused you to say, "That would really help me," that's the one to pick. If you have a self-sabotaging habit that none of these Desserts addresses, make up your own to help you start changing that habit.

Record your Dessert as the last Daily Action on your Action Work-sheet (see Figure 5-2).

Time for the Main Course

The Daily Actions in the Main Course section of the menu are activities directly aimed at getting you clients. The Main Course items are grouped into categories that match the stages of the Universal Marketing Cycle: filling the pipeline, following up, getting presentations, and closing sales. Because the possible activities for filling the pipeline are so varied, that area is subdivided into six sections, based on the marketing strategies each activity uses:

- Direct contact and follow-up
- Networking and referral building
- Public speaking
- Writing and publicity
- Promotional events
- Advertising

You will be selecting seven or eight Daily Actions from the Main Course menu (or of your own design), to reach a total of ten Daily Actions all together. The first rule to follow in making your choices is this: Don't read the whole list! Look solely at the category that pertains to the mar-keting cycle stage you are working on. If your chosen stage is filling the pipeline, look only at the sections relevant to the marketing strategies you have chosen.

Icons that indicate which of the six Get Clients Now! marketing strategies each activity is related to appear on the left-hand side of the menu. For a key to the strategy icons, refer to Chapter 4. Some actions are applicable to only one strategy, while others could relate to several, depending on how they are used.

Here are two different approaches to making your selections:

1. Just pick 'em. As you have worked your way through the exercises in this book, you have already learned quite a bit about marketing. You know where in the Universal Marketing Cycle you are stuck or need more work, what marketing strategies you plan to use, and which missing ingredients you need to be successful. Maybe you already have enough information about possible marketing tactics to choose some from the Daily Actions listed for your marketing cycle stage. When you are ready to begin using your selected actions, you can read more about them in the marketing recipes in Part III of the book.

2. First understand the theory. Each Daily Action on the list represents an activity that has been proven effective in professional services marketing. Sometimes the purpose of an activity will be immediately apparent. It's difficult to misunderstand what "spend 1 hour each day cold calling" is about. Other activities are more subtle. For example, "have lunch or coffee with a center of influence once per week" is listed for closing sales because this activity will simultaneously increase your visibility and credibility. When a prospective client hears about you from someone she respects, it can greatly increase your likelihood of closing the sale.

If you want to understand more about the purpose of the Main Course activities before making your choices, read the specific chapter in Part III of this book that describes your chosen stage of the marketing cycle. You can skip any sections that relate to marketing strategies you will not be using.

Is one of these approaches to selecting Main Course actions more successful than the other? Actually, no—the difference is in you. If you are comfortable shooting from the hip, use the first approach. It's quicker and easier. If you don't like to commit to a course of action until you have thoroughly evaluated your choices, use the second approach. It will increase your level of commitment to the actions you choose.

How to Make the Best Selections

Here are the questions you should consider to make the best possible choices from the Main Course menu:

- *Where are you stuck or in need of more work?* You already know which stage of the Universal Marketing Cycle you need to focus on, so choose only Main Course items that pertain to that stage. If you don't see seven or eight actions that seem right to you on the list for your stage, it's fine to take one or two actions from the stage just before or after yours.

The Main Thing Is . . .

Zig Ziglar is the author of 24 books on sales and success, including the classic *Secrets of Closing the Sale* (Berkley, 1985). In *Staying Up, Up, Up in a Down, Down World* (Nelson, 2004), Zig comments, "The refrain most often heard in the media, in private conversations and correspondence, is 'I apologize for not getting back sooner, but I've been so busy.'

"The question is, are we really busier than we've ever been? In reality, based on what 10,000 people recorded in their hour-by-hour time diaries, Americans, on the average, have 40 hours a week of discretionary time which they can invest as they please. This is more than they had 30 years ago and five hours more than they had in 1975.

"The basic problem is that today we have so many options as to how we spend our leisure time that we jump from one activity to another, never spending any significant amount of time doing the one thing which would actually bring us more enjoyment.

"Combine that with the fact that today, our evaluation of the importance of leisure time has gone up substantially. A [poll in] *U.S. News & World Report* showed that 49 percent of Americans [versus 28 percent in 1986] believe that society needs to stop emphasizing work and put more value on 'free time.'

"I'm convinced that much of this feeling is because we have lost our ability to concentrate on what we're doing. Many people while on the job spend too much time thinking about their home life and when they're at home they spend too much time thinking about their jobs.

"It's impossible to completely focus on the job for eight hours; your mind naturally moves to other things. But you need to 'keep the main thing the main thing,' and while you're at work, your work is the main thing. When you're at home, family is the main thing."

Zig Ziglar
www.ziglar.com

However, don't pick actions from several different stages. This will dilute your marketing efforts and sabotage the Persistence Effect.

- *Which marketing strategies are you using?* The icons shown for each action indicate what marketing strategy they relate to. Look for the actions that match up with the strategies you chose in Chapter 2. In each marketing cycle stage, you'll find that a majority of the Main Course actions support the strategies of direct contact and follow-up, and networking and referral building, because this is where the Persistence Effect has the most impact. For some of the other strategies, fewer choices are available. If you want to include more actions that support some of the other strategies, feel free to make up some of your own. For example, if you chose promotional events as a strategy, you could design more action steps focused on launching the specific type of event you have in mind. Remember, though, that you may have already chosen Success Ingredients that address those areas as well.

If you are working on filling the pipeline, you may wonder why there are fewer actions listed under direct contact and follow-up than there are under networking and referral building. After all, isn't direct contact supposed to be the most effective strategy? While this is certainly true overall, keep in mind that your objective in filling the pipeline is to locate qualified prospects with whom you can quickly close sales. Making a completely cold approach by researching, calling, and mailing people you do not know is much less effective than being connected to them via introduction, referral, speaking, etc. So when filling the pipeline, a better approach is to couple direct contact activities with networking and other strategies to warm up your approaches.

- *What will you actually do?* If you are paralyzed by cold calling or public speaking, there is no point in including these actions in your program, because you will simply avoid doing them. You might choose a Success Ingredient to help you improve your future skills in these areas, but the Daily Actions you pick need to be activities you are willing to do this month. Instead of choosing actions you could find immobilizing, ask yourself . . .

- *What are you naturally drawn to?* If you are typically outgoing and enjoy talking to people, choose actions that will get you to networking events and give you plenty of time on the phone. But if talking to strangers makes you so uncomfortable that you will do anything to avoid it, select actions that will allow you to concentrate on building referrals with people you already know or writing articles for publication.

If you choose activities you like, or are at least willing to try, you will do them.

• *How much available time do you have?* If you are full-time in your business but have few or no clients, you may have quite a bit of time available for marketing. You may be able to spend as much time market-ing as you would working for your clients. But if you have another job or are busy with client work, you will have to fit your marketing activities into what may be an already full week. Time constraints may require you to conduct more of your marketing by phone or online than in person, or during evenings and weekends. Make sure your choices reflect the real-ity of your situation.

• *How soon do you need to produce results?* The sooner you need to find more clients, the more aggressive your marketing action plan should be. If your situation—financial or emotional—is becoming desperate, choose actions that are ambitious enough to accelerate your progress.

To make your selections, look at the section of the Main Course menu that corresponds to your stage of the marketing cycle. Place a check mark next to each Daily Action that seems to fit your situation. It's all right to

---

Nobody Wants a Drudger

"If you're not having any fun doing what you do, think back to a time when you were," suggests business and personal coach Cat Williford. "What 'drudge' do you currently have that wasn't there when you were having fun? How can you eliminate the drudge when you are marketing your business?

"When you're not having any fun in your marketing, you are wasting your time, which just adds to the drudge. Don't you want to do business with people who seem to enjoy life and what they do for a living? If you wouldn't want to do business with yourself, *you* may be the problem in your marketing!

"If you can eliminate the drudge by having fun when you market yourself, you will draw to you the type of clients you really want."

Cat Williford, MCC, CPCC
www.cocreativealliance.com

pick some actions that are easy for you or that you are already doing consistently, but you should also choose some that will stretch and challenge you.

If you end up with too many activities, ask yourself which ones would make the most efficient use of your time. What do you think will bring you the most return with the least effort? And remember: It doesn't matter so much what you choose as it does *that* you choose. Everything on the menu works.

When you have selected your seven or eight Main Course actions for a total of ten Daily Actions overall, adjust the quantity and frequency of each one to suit you. Then write them on your Action Worksheet as in Figure 5-2.

A Word About Closing Sales

If you are working on filling the pipeline or following up, it may have occurred to you to wonder how you are actually going to make a sale. After all, the Daily Actions on your list are all focused on the earlier stages in the marketing cycle.

The key word to understanding the answer is *focus*. You have chosen to concentrate your effort on a particular stage of the marketing cycle because that is where you are feeling stuck or need more work. This doesn't mean, however, that you should ignore the routine functions of the other stages while you are doing this. If your pipeline-filling activities turn up a hot lead, follow up immediately. If your follow-up generates a presentation, make it. If your presentation leads to closing the sale, great! That's what you want.

Your Daily Actions in the program are in no way intended to be a list of everything you must do about marketing and sales for the next month. You need to continue pursuing solid leads with the same energy you always have (or perhaps a little more, because now you have a goal to meet). The intent of the Daily Actions is simply to focus more effort on the area of your marketing that needs it the most.

The Get Clients Now! program should hold the same place in your marketing and sales activities as an exercise program does in your life. You don't quit walking to the bus stop because you are now doing twenty-five sit-ups each morning, and you don't stop playing ball with the kids because you decide to run a mile three times a week. Routine life goes on while you are exercising; regular selling goes on while you are improving your performance in the areas of pipeline-filling and follow-up.

Marketing Alone Won't Do It

Howard Shenson, the "consultant's consultant," published over sixty books, reports, and other tools for consultants during his lifetime. In his guide *Shenson on Consulting* (Wiley, 1994), he points out: "Consultants must engage in both marketing and selling to build viable practices. Success requires that the professional understand the difference between these two promotional activities. Marketing involves all activities that are designed to establish the image and reputation of the consultant and to make the market aware of the availability of his or her services. The opportunity to sell results from successful marketing and involves all activities that cause an interested prospect to engage the services of the consultant. Some professionals feel that they need do only one or the other, or they cannot see the fine distinction between the two. Both are vital . . .

"Client awareness of and appreciation for the image and reputation of a particular consultant can be created through either indirect, public-relations-type marketing activities or direct marketing strategies or both. But even the best and most effective marketing does not eliminate the need for selling, for selling involves the art of demonstrating to an interested and informed client the wisdom of engaging the professional's services and allows the professional the opportunity to customize and particularize in relation to the prospect's specific needs."

Howard L. Shenson, CMC
1944–1991

What Is Going to Stop You?

Look at what you have recorded on your Action Worksheet. You have an ambitious goal, Success Ingredients you are going to acquire or create, and a list of ten Daily Actions you are going to perform, all in the next twenty-eight days. If looking at this list makes you feel resistant, afraid, or overwhelmed, your reaction is completely normal.

If you have ever attempted a program before—dieting or regular exercise, for example—or taken a motivational seminar, or made some New

Year's resolutions, you have probably experienced the following familiar scenario. You make new commitments when you are feeling enthusiastic, reenergized, or just plain fed up with the way things are. But then something stops you from following through.

What is that something? Lack of time—and its frequent companion, not enough money—are easy excuses, but the fact is that most of us make choices every day about where to spend our time and money. We choose whether to make a cold call or chat with a friend, pay the admission price to a networking event or buy a movie ticket. And it's not just choosing between work and play. Suddenly, deleting all the old e-mails in your inbox may seem more important than writing a marketing letter, or spending money on a new cell phone becomes more urgent than paying to have your website updated.

If you are really serious about making this time different, about following through on your commitments and getting the results you want, it's time to look at what may get in your way. Are you worried or afraid? If so, of what? Are you resisting something? What is it? Is there some special permission that you need in order to be successful with this program?

Many people, if not most people, are routinely blocked in marketing and sales by self-sabotaging thinking or behavior. If you thought you were the only one suffering from terminal procrastination or struggling with negative messages from your own inner critic, know you're in good company. Giving yourself permission to alter a long-standing habit can be a powerful step in the direction of lasting change. In the Get Clients Now! program, you will be consciously granting yourself a Special Permission every day. Here are some examples:

I have permission to ask for what I want.

I am able to do things I fear.

I deserve to be successful.

I can make a good living and still have time for fun.

The best way to design a Special Permission is to ask yourself what you routinely think or do that prevents you from being successful at marketing. For example, suppose you never seem to have time to make follow-up calls because you are busy working on client projects. You know this behavior backfires in the long run, because when you complete a project, there isn't another one waiting for you. The permission you might design for yourself is, "It's okay to put my marketing first."

Got Permission from a Rabbit

"I joined a Get Clients Now! group years ago when I needed to expand my business," remembers coach and professional organizer Shannon Seek. "In my false sense of courage I didn't even know I had fear at first, but I felt stuck. During the program, I recognized that I needed to give myself permission to be afraid. I came up with a metaphor that would help me visualize it: 'Be the bunny.' On the Native American medicine wheel, the rabbit represents fear, and working with Rabbit Medicine requires owning your fear when you have it.

"I imagined myself as a rabbit hopping through fear—timid-but-still-moving bunny—or a rabbit in a World War I fighter plane with goggles and ears flopping in the wind—fearless bunny. It made being fearful seem funny, safe, and okay enough that I could deal with the task at hand. It really got me unstuck."

Shannon Seek, CPCC
www.seeksolutions.com

Or, suppose that you are stalling in completing your portfolio, because then you will actually have to show it to someone. And if you did so, he or she might not like your work. Of course, you also know that if you don't show your portfolio to anyone, it's unlikely that anyone will hire you. In this case, you might choose this Special Permission: "I believe in my talents and abilities."

Are you wondering what is going to make you believe your Special Permission? After all, you just made it up. What will make it real for you? For one thing, there is the simple repetition of it. Repetition is one of the primary ways that we learn. You learned the alphabet by heart from saying or singing it over and over. If you look in the mirror each morning and say, "I believe in my talents and abilities," you will begin to internalize that information in the same way that you know "F" comes before "G" without reciting the alphabet from the beginning.

The other reason your Special Permission will work is that it's only for twenty-eight days. Whenever you find yourself questioning the validity of your permission, remind yourself it is only temporary. You can go back to your old way of operating at the end of the month (if you still want to). Just as Samuel T. Coleridge's expression "the willing suspension of disbelief" can be the key to enjoying a novel or play, you can temporarily allow yourself to believe fully in your Special Permission. If you are skeptical, try it.

If you already know your Special Permission, write it on the last line of your Action Worksheet. If you're still having trouble finding a permission that fits, just pick one of the previous examples to start with. It's almost a guarantee that some block or obstacle will appear within the first few days of starting the program. Then you can design a new Special Permission to address it. And if at any point during the twenty-eight days your permission stops working for you, change it.

Chapter 6

You're Ready . . . Let's Go!
Putting the System into Action

"Whatever you can do, or dream you can, begin it. Boldness has genius, power, and magic in it."

—Goethe

The Tracking Worksheet

Your Action Worksheet is completed. You have chosen your Program Goal, one to three Success Ingredients, ten Daily Actions, and your Special Permission. It's time to put your own personal Get Clients Now! program into action.

Your second essential tool for the twenty-eight days of the program is the Tracking Worksheet, which you will use daily to measure your progress through the program. The Tracking Worksheet is quite a magical device. You will be amazed at how much difference this one little piece of paper can make in your marketing!

Remember the benefits of goal-setting discussed in Chapter 3? Using the Tracking Worksheet consistently will automatically provide you with focus, evidence, direction, and motivation for your marketing. If you arrange to work through the program with a buddy, group, or coach, you will also lock in place the accountability, perspective, and support to help you succeed.

Look at Lee Greenback's partially completed Tracking Worksheet in Figure 6-1. Each column represents a working day of the program, for which you will make daily entries like these:

Weather Report. On a one-to-ten scale, with one being the lowest and ten the highest, how is your state of mind today? How does your

Figure 6-1 Partially Completed Tracking Worksheet

GET CLIENTS NOW!™

Tracking Worksheet

Start Date: 10/02/06

Name: Lee Greenback

	10/2	10/3	10/4	10/5	10/6	10/9	10/10	10/11	10/12	10/13	10/16	10/17	10/18	10/19	10/20	10/23	10/24	10/25	10/26	10/27
Weather Report (1-10 scale)																				
Mind	8	7	8	9	8															
Body	7	7	8	8	7															
Success Ingredients (% done)																				
1 mkt niche definition - 10/6	50	50	75	75	100															
2 10-second intro - 10/13	25	25	25	25	50															
3 3 networking venues - 10/20	0	0	0	33	33															
Daily/Weekly Actions (Y/N)																				
1 1/2 hour/day on SI project	N	N	Y	Y	Y															
2 ltrs/e-mails to 6 people/wk	Y	Y	N	Y	Y															
3 warm calls to 2 prospects/day	Y	Y	Y	Y	N															
4 1 networking event/wk	Y	Y	Y	Y	Y															
5 3 new referral partners/wk	Y	Y	Y	Y	Y															
6 lunch/coffee w/colleague wkly	Y	Y	Y	Y	Y															
7 3 message board posts/wk	Y	Y	Y	Y	Y															
8 item to 3 colleagues/wk	Y	Y	Y	Y	Y															
9 ask for referral 1/day	N	N	N	Y	Y															
10 visualize success daily	Y	Y	N	Y	Y															
Total (# of 10)	8	8	7	10	9															
Program Goal (% of target)																				
4 new clients	0	0	0	0	25															
Special Permission (Y/N)																				
enough time for everything	Y	Y	N	Y	Y															

body feel? This is an intuitive score; put down what you sense is correct. These numbers will go up and down from day to day, as your mood and physical condition fluctuate. This score tells you how much you should expect from yourself on any given day.

Success Ingredients. For each of your one to three Success Ingredient projects, what percentage have you completed? If zero percent means you have done nothing thus far and 100 percent means the project is done, how far do you estimate that you have progressed along the range? This too may be an intuitive score, or for some projects you can compute it mathematically. These numbers will go up as projects move forward, but will not go down.

Daily/Weekly Actions. For each of your ten actions, did you do it today (Y) or not (N)? At the bottom of this section, record the total number of actions completed at the end of each day. This number will increase or decrease from day to day as your productivity varies and other activities require your attention.

When an action is weekly (or several times per week) rather than daily, you should still score yourself for that action each day. In this case, your score will depend on how well you carry out your plans. Let's say you have chosen the action "Go to 1 networking event each week." When it's time to score yourself for this action on Monday, if you planned to attend an event today and you went, give yourself a Y. If you planned to attend one today and didn't go, you get an N. If you didn't plan to go to an event today at all, you get a free Y, but you should look at your calendar now and decide what day you will attend one this week. Then score yourself each day based on how well you followed through on your intention. Whenever you get to the end of the week and still haven't taken a weekly action, you must give yourself an N for it on Friday. Be honest and remember—these scores are for you.

Program Goal. What percentage of your goal have you achieved so far? Since all goals in the program must be numerical, you should be able to compute this exactly. This number will increase as your goals move forward, but will not decrease.

Special Permission. Do you have your Special Permission today or not? Tell the truth. You will notice how difficult everything is on those days you don't have it.

On Day One of the program, you will start filling in your own Tracking Worksheet, based on the Action Worksheet you completed at the end of Chapter 5.

The 28-Day Program

For the next twenty-eight days, you will be working steadily on achieving your chosen marketing goal. But if you keep your foot on the accelerator the whole time, you will run out of gas!

You should plan ahead which days you will be working on your marketing and which days you will rest. There are rest days built into the program so you can have time to regroup and recharge. You may choose to spend some of a rest day working on a Success Ingredient project or the exercises in this chapter, but you will be responsible for completing your Daily Actions only on the days you have chosen as working days. In the program outline that follows, your working days are scheduled Monday through Friday, and your rest days are assumed to be back to back, on Saturday and Sunday. If your work week is different, you will need to adjust the program days to fit your actual schedule.

On your program working days, you should set aside in advance time to complete your Daily Actions, especially if you are already busy with client work or have another job. You may need to plan for some of your marketing activities to take place before or after the business day, or during lunch. Experiment to find the best time of day to fit these tasks into your schedule. Don't let the work you already have be your excuse for not finding the clients you really need. Make marketing your first priority instead of the last thing you do.

On working and rest days alike, read the entry for each day from the pages that follow. Try to do this as early in the day as possible so that you will keep your marketing in mind throughout the course of the day. On each working day, you should also spend a few moments doing a morning review to plan how you will include your Success Ingredient projects, Daily Actions, and your Special Permission in the day's agenda. At the end of each working day, take another few moments to add up your daily scores on the Tracking Worksheet. There are more details about these activities in the pages that follow.

On some of the rest days there are exercises provided to help you be more effective and productive in your marketing. To get the most benefit from the program, be sure to set aside some time to work with each of these, whether or not it is on the day suggested.

DAY 1

Saturday is a great day to begin your Get Clients Now! program. Close the door, turn off the phone, and bring out your completed Action Worksheet from Chapter 5. Make an enlarged copy of the blank Tracking Worksheet in Figure 6-2, or download the worksheet from the book's companion website at www.getclientsnow.com. Fill in the dates on the top line and the information in Column One. See Lee Greenback's partially completed worksheet (Figure 6-1) for an example.

On the top line, write the calendar dates of your working days for the next month. If the coming Monday were October 2, for example, you would label the first ten columns on your worksheet 10/2–10/6 and 10/9–10/13, skipping the Saturday and Sunday rest days in between. Next, write in Column One the Success Ingredients from your Action Worksheet with your chosen target dates. Then add your ten Daily Actions, Program Goal, and Special Permission.

Award yourself a starting score on each of your Success Ingredients and your Program Goal. Are you starting from zero on your Success Ingredient projects and the goal you set for the month, or have you already made some progress? On Lee Greenback's worksheet, he gave himself a starting score of 50 percent on "market niche definition," believing he was already halfway there. On his "10-second introduction," he had done some work, but needed more, so he scored himself at 25 percent. For "networking venues," Lee had yet to do anything, so he started at zero.

To give yourself an accurate score now and throughout the program, you may need to quantify your Success Ingredient projects. For Success Ingredients like "networking venues" or "referral partners," consider the question, "How many is enough?" If you're unsure, review the appropriate chapter in Part III for your chosen stage of the Universal Marketing Cycle. Write the number you choose on your worksheet, as Lee did for his networking venues. If you have chosen a more intangible Success Ingredient, such as "networking skills" or "telemarketing skills," score yourself intuitively. If zero equals "phone phobic" and 100 percent means "expert telemarketer," where would you rate yourself today? Would you like to be at 100 percent by the end of the program, or would 75 percent satisfy you? If it's the latter, write down "telemarketing skills at 75 percent," so you know what you're aiming for.

Now award yourself a starting score on your Program Goal. As described in Chapter 3, this is a numerical target for clients, contracts, appointments, billable hours, total revenue, or new prospects. You may be starting at zero, or you may have made some progress already. Either way, be honest with yourself, and be specific about what you are count-

Figure 6-2 Blank Tracking Worksheet

GET CLIENTS NOW!™ Tracking Worksheet																													
Weather Report (1-10 scale)																													
Mind																													
Body																													
Success Ingredients (% done)																													
1																													
2																													
3																													
Daily/Weekly Actions (Y/N)																													
1																													
2																													
3																													
4																													
5																													
6																													
7																													
8																													
9																													
10																													
Total (# of 10)																													
Program Goal (% of target)																													
Special Permission (Y/N)																													

Start Date: _____

Name: _____

ing. Is a new client anyone who schedules his first appointment, or does this count only after the person shows up for it? Is your total revenue what you bill this month, or what you actually collect? Base your score on a way of measuring that will make this goal truly meaningful for you.

Now put the Tracking Worksheet where you will be sure to see it first thing Monday morning. Are you ready to make a commitment to the program you have designed for yourself?

Thought for the day: Jay Conrad Levinson, author of the *Guerrilla Marketing* series, often says the following when asked about his work: "I hate to admit this, but mediocre marketing with commitment works better than brilliant marketing without commitment."

DAY 2

Rest Day. Do something you really enjoy, perhaps an activity you haven't had time for in a while. You're going to be working hard for the next month, so take this opportunity to have some fun. Get plenty of sleep tonight so you'll be fresh and ready to go in the morning.

Thought for the day: Even God rested one day a week.

DAY 3

Are you ready to get clients now? It's time to let the Tracking Worksheet start doing its magic. First thing this morning place your Tracking Worksheet in front of you. Each working day of the program, you will be using the worksheet at least twice: once at the beginning and once at the end of the day. To let even more of the worksheet's magic rub off on you, post it where you'll see it all day long.

On this first Monday, begin by doing your first Morning Review. Look over your Success Ingredients and Daily Actions. Which of these tasks do you plan to work on today? Do you need to add them to your daily to-do list or schedule time for them? Check your Special Permission to remind yourself what you need to be successful. Okay, you're ready for the day—go for it!

At day's end, award yourself your first Daily Scores:

Weather Report: Your mind and body on a scale of one to ten.

Success Ingredients: The status of each project from 0–100 percent complete.

Daily/Weekly Actions: Y (for Yes) and N (for No) on each one. Add up the total number of Ys at the bottom.

Program Goal: Progress toward your goal from 0–100 percent accomplished.

Special Permission: Y if you granted yourself your Special Permission today; N if you didn't.

If you have questions about how to score yourself, refer to the description of the Tracking Worksheet at the beginning of this chapter.

You made it through your first working day of the Get Clients Now! program—congratulations! Did you accomplish all that you wanted? If you did, great! If not, we'll look at your list again tomorrow to see if you need to make changes. Throughout the remainder of the program, the day-by-day guidelines here will focus on keeping you in action, on track, and motivated. Whenever you have questions about how to implement the Daily Actions or Success Ingredients you chose, refer to the appropriate chapter in Part III for your stage of the marketing cycle to find detailed logistical help.

Thought for the day: A short poem about marketing:

You have to sow a lot of seeds.

Some are flowers; some are weeds;

Some will die while others grow,

But all depends on how many you sow.

DAY 4

Begin the day with your Morning Review. Look at your Success Ingredients, Daily Actions, and Special Permission and plan how you will include each in the day's agenda. You will do this each working day of the program. In today's review, and for all of this first week, pay special attention to the Daily Actions you chose. How did it work for you to add these new activities into your day?

If you scored eight or above on your Daily Actions yesterday, keep them as they are. If you scored lower, but yesterday was unusually busy or chaotic, give yourself another day to see how you do. However, if you're feeling overwhelmed and suspect that your choices may have been too ambitious, you have complete permission to scale back a bit. Rather than eliminating any of the actions you chose, try just reducing the level of effort. Is there something you committed to do daily that could happen three times per week instead? Or could you cut down on the number of calls, letters, or meetings you had planned? Now is the time to redesign a list of actions that will work for you within the reality of a normal day.

At the end of the day, compile your Daily Scores. Did you do better today? Terrific! If you're still not satisfied with your scores, don't worry; we will continue to look at ways of making them improve.

Thought for the day: You will never be completely ready. Start from wherever you are.

DAY 5

Morning Review. Wednesday is the day to look at any once-per-week actions that have yet to be scheduled. Choose now the day you will do them. If a lunch or meeting is involved, lock it in place by calling to make the appointment or reservation.

Daily Scores. Have you reached a score of eight or higher on your Daily Actions? If so, good work! Try setting up a reward for yourself if you reach a certain score tomorrow. If today's score was six, go for a score of eight; if nine was your score today, make tomorrow's goal a ten.

Thought for the day: Everyone you meet is either a prospect or a potential source of referrals. Never pass up an opportunity to introduce yourself.

DAY 6

Morning Review. What will be your reward if you reach your Daily Actions target today? What do you need to do to make that score possible? Here are three suggested strategies to try:

1. *Do it first.* Avoid doing anything else until your Daily Actions are completed. Don't check your e-mail, tidy up the house, or answer the phone. Eliminate every possible distraction until you have reached your target score for today.

2. *Do it now.* You may have some Daily Actions that need to occur later in your day rather than first thing. Every time you think of one of them, do it immediately. Let's say you need to ask for one referral per day. When you are in conversation with someone, just ask for a referral as soon as you think of it—right then, no matter what you are talking about. If you find yourself forgetting, put a rubber band around your wrist, and let it remind you each time you notice it.

3. *Block out time.* If your schedule prevents doing all your Daily Actions first, block out time on your calendar. Make a specific appointment with yourself and honor it just as though someone else was expecting you. Use this appointment as an excuse if other people try to detain you. If you're afraid you'll forget or get busy with something else, try setting an alarm.

Daily Scores. Did you earn your reward today? Congratulations! If you're still having trouble, review your Daily Actions list again. If you find it too ambitious, you can scale back your level of effort at any point during the program, as long as you stick to the guidelines for choosing Daily Actions given in Chapter 5. You may decide that you already have the right list, but the problem you need to solve is how to make it happen. Try again tomorrow to use the three strategies listed above. It may take you several attempts to successfully change your work habits so that marketing becomes a part of your day. Keep at it; the payoff will be worth the effort.

Thought for the day: Learning any new habit is like starting an exercise program: It can be painful at first, but as you exercise that particular muscle, it becomes stronger and supports you better. Over time, the pain gives way to tolerance, tolerance to satisfaction, and satisfaction to exhilaration as you see the results of your commitment and persistence.

DAY 7

Morning Review. It's your last chance to complete any actions scheduled as weekly, so look now at how to fit them in. What Daily Actions score will you go for today?

Daily Scores. How did you do this week? If you got your Daily Actions score up to eight or more, it's time to celebrate your achievement. You are on the path to success in reaching your Program Goal and getting more clients. If your scores are in the five to seven range, you are getting close, but need to make some changes. Revisit the Morning Review for Days Four and Six to see what else you might do. If you are consistently scoring lower than five on Daily Actions, you are not failing, you are learning. There is something in your way, and once you know what it is, you can begin to eliminate it. We'll look at some of these potential roadblocks tomorrow.

Complete your week by making a list of your wins over the last seven days. What worked? What went well? What great things did you do, say, receive, and achieve? Here's a sample "wins" list:

- Completed my 10-second introduction and tried it out at a networking event
- Met three potential referral partners at the Association of Accounting Professionals meeting
- Studied two chapters of a book about networking
- Had lunch with my former boss and got some inside info on local firms

- Read about two companies that might need my services in this month's issue of *Accounting Pro*
- Heard that the Helping Hand Foundation might need a volunteer accountant

Put your wins list where you can see it, right next to your Tracking Worksheet. Then congratulate yourself—you stuck with the program through Week One.

Thought for the day: There are benefits of doing business with you that you take for granted but that would thrill your prospects if they knew about them. Look for the hidden assets in your business, and be sure to reveal them in your marketing.

DAY 8

Rest Day. In the first week of the Get Clients Now! program, you may have encountered two of the biggest obstacles to marketing success: fear and resistance. If looking at some of the items on your Daily Actions list made your stomach flutter or your throat get tight, that was fear. If you found yourself thinking, "I don't want to . . ." and digging in your heels, that was resistance. Know that you are not alone in these feelings. You may not hear other folks talk about this at the Chamber of Commerce, but most people feel afraid, resistant, or both, about certain elements of marketing.

Identifying the source of these feelings and why you have them is beyond the scope of this book. What you need now is to get past them in order to be successful—and you can! The first step in removing these roadblocks is to recognize they exist; then be specific about their nature. Answer these questions now:

1. *What are you afraid of?* Being rejected? Making a mistake? Failing? Succeeding? Looking silly? Write down as many different fears as you can. If you feel stuck, ask yourself, "What do I think would happen if I . . ." and complete the sentence with whatever Daily Actions are giving you trouble—perhaps ". . . went to a networking event?" or ". . . made a cold call?"

2. *What are you resisting?* Doing the work? Bragging about your abilities? Spending time on marketing when you have other urgent priorities? Finish this sentence in your best whining voice, "I don't want to . . ."

Now that these barriers are out in the open, ask yourself if you are going to let them stop you. They don't have to, you know. You can feel afraid yet move forward; you can feel resistant yet still do what you are resisting. The next time you are having trouble, notice what you are feeling, and choose whether to let it keep you from taking action. Say to yourself, "Oh, there's the fear again," or "Wow, I'm really feeling resistant right now" and then keep going.

Thought for the day: Courage is not the absence of fear. It is the ability to take action while feeling afraid.

DAY 9

Rest Day. Reward yourself for a week well done. Spend an entire day not thinking about work. Do something relaxing and replenishing.

Thought for the day: You are the biggest asset your business has. Taking care of yourself is taking care of business.

DAY 10

Morning Review. Continue planning your day to include all your Daily Actions and try for a daily score of eight or higher. In this second week, we will shift the focus to your Success Ingredient projects. How has your progress been here? You are one-fourth of the way through the program, so you should be 25 percent ahead of where you started on your Success Ingredients. If you are working on three simultaneously, each should have progressed that far. If you are doing them in succession, the first should be near completion.

Daily Scores. Were you able to give your Success Ingredients enough attention today? Look now at the rest of your week, and see where you can fit them in. In order to stay on track, you should be halfway through by Friday.

Thought for the day: Work expands to fill the time allotted to it. If you want to get more done, give each task only the amount of time it is worth to you. And if you want to work less, allow less time for work.

DAY 11

Morning Review. Are you having trouble finding enough time for your Success Ingredients? If you are on or ahead of schedule, good for you! If not, here are some strategies to help:

1. *Give something away.* What else is currently on your to-do list? Is there anything you can hand off to someone else? If you can't unload an entire project, are there some pieces you could ask another person to do?

If you are unaccustomed to delegating, you may need to expand your vision of what it looks like. You don't necessarily need an administrative assistant in order to delegate; you can delegate to a co-worker, a colleague, a friend, your spouse or partner, your children, your siblings, another committee member, or a paid professional. What are you doing that someone else could do instead? Can you ask someone else? Can you pay someone else? If it enabled you to spend an extra hour a day on marketing, could you afford to pay someone to handle some of your responsibilities?

2. *Put something off.* What on your list can be done later? If you have a habit of planning more things than you can possibly do, you are already putting some things off by default. Why not choose up front what those things will be? Think in terms of your overall priorities. What is more important than marketing? There will certainly be a few things, such as servicing your current clients or spending some time with your family, but it's unlikely that everything on your list is more important than marketing right now. Find some tasks that you can defer for the next seventeen days.

3. *Let something go.* If you have had a task on your list for several weeks and not gotten it done, does it truly require doing? If you haven't made time for it in this long, how important can it be? Try this: cross it off the list for one week, and see if it comes back to haunt you. If you can forget about it, that's one less thing to do. If you can't let it drop, revisit the first two options above.

Daily Scores. Did you make more headway on Success Ingredients today? What will be your target scores for tomorrow?

Thought for the day: Market research surveys indicate that the average American is exposed to over one million marketing messages per year. Remember that when you're wondering if it's too soon to follow up with someone who has heard from you before.

DAY 12

Morning Review. You have three days left to hit the 50 percent mark on your Success Ingredients. What will it take? If you are having any logistical challenges or how-to questions, read the chapter in Part III that discusses the marketing cycle stage you are working on.

Daily Scores. Did you hit your target scores? Take a moment to celebrate! Are you still struggling? You may need some additional support. Call your business buddy or a friend and ask that person to help you in the following specific way:

1. *Set a fixed time to talk*. Whether you meet by phone or in person, set a start and end time for your conversation. This will tighten the focus on solving your problem. Half an hour is probably enough; an hour is plenty.

2. *Begin by clearing*. Ask your buddy to just listen while you recount what's going on. Your buddy can say things like, "Gee, that's tough," or "How awful!" but should avoid offering advice until you have told the whole story. Talk about not only what is happening, but also how it makes you feel. If it sounds like complaining, that probably means you're doing it right. You might be saying something like: "I've been trying for two weeks to finish the new copy for my website but there's just been one emergency after another, and now my mother wants me to help with getting her computer fixed, and I'm so frustrated! All the words I write down just come out wrong, and I don't think it'll ever come together, and I needed it yesterday, and I'm so worried that . . ." You get the idea.

Set a time limit of five to ten minutes for clearing. Then ask your buddy to summarize for you: "I hear how frustrated and worried you are. You seem to have two problems that need to be solved: finding the time to work on the website copy, and getting the words to come out right. Are you ready to look at some solutions?"

3. *Brainstorm possible solutions*. Now that your problems are out in the open, you can get some assistance in solving them. Your buddy's job is not to hand you the right answer; it is to help you expand your thinking to come up with some new ideas. Take your problems one at time and together with your buddy make a list of possible solutions. Don't edit the list as you are brainstorming; you will do that later. Anything and everything that comes up should go on the list. A basic principle of brainstorming is that you are not allowed to say, "That won't work," or "I already tried that." Here are the potential results of a brainstorm aimed at getting the right words for your website:

- Hire a copywriter
- Plagiarize my competitors' sites
- Use a thesaurus
- Ask my cousin, the writer, to help
- Design a website with pictures instead of words
- Don't have a website at all
- Look at sites I like for inspiration

- Take a class in copywriting
- Leave the site like it is and stop worrying
- Have some colleagues review it

4. *Look for a next step.* You can ask your buddy to help you with this or do it later on your own. If none of the brainstormed ideas seems right, look at each one to see if there's something useful in it. Maybe you can't afford a copywriter, but you know one you could ask for some free advice. Perhaps a class in copywriting would take too long, but you could buy an e-book on the subject and read it tonight. Find just one thing you can do that will get you moving forward again.

Thought for the day: It really doesn't matter what you choose; the important thing is *that* you choose.

DAY 13

Morning Review. Set a target for your Success Ingredient scores today that is a no-kidding-whatever-it-takes goal. Remember that you said you needed these things to be successful.

Daily Scores. Did you make it? Congratulations! Not quite there? You have one more day to catch up. Take a moment to remind yourself of your Special Permission. Did you have it today? If not, what do you need to do, say, or believe to grant yourself that permission? Now that you have been working with the program for a while, is there any other needed permission you have discovered? It's okay to switch, or even have two of them if that serves you in moving forward.

Thought for the day: If some people don't say your price is too high, you're not charging enough.

DAY 14

Morning Review. It's the halfway point in your Get Clients Now! program. Where do you want to be at the end of the day?

Daily Scores. You have worked diligently this week so pat yourself on the back. If you achieved your target scores on Daily Actions and Success Ingredients, you are on your way to a successful conclusion by month's end. If you are unhappy with your performance, consider how much more you have accomplished in these two weeks than before you started the program. If you have yet to reach the 50 percent mark with your Success Ingredients, revisit Day Eleven's Morning Review or schedule another call with your buddy to see what else you might do.

Complete your week by making and posting your wins list. Hooray! You made it through Week Two!

Thought for the day: There is no failure, only feedback.

DAY 15

Rest Day. During Week Two, it's a good bet that you found yourself having at least one conversation with your inner critic. Also known as "the committee," or negative self-talk, this is the self-defeating voice you hear in your head that says: "You're not good enough," "You don't know how," and "They won't like me." The inner critic often has much to say about sales and marketing. This is a place in your life where you are putting yourself on the line, often bringing up all your concerns with being inadequate. Negative self-talk is one of the biggest obstacles you must overcome to achieve success.

Everyone has an inner critic (yes, everyone!), but some people manage it better than others. It is possible to manage it so well that you hardly notice it. To begin managing your inner critic, here are some steps to follow:

1. *Raise your awareness.* Every time you find yourself fearful, nervous, hesitant, or second-guessing, stop and notice what is happening. You may have a particular behavior pattern that manifests itself when the inner critic is active, such as procrastinating, avoiding people or tasks, or being distracted by trivial interruptions. Or there may be a body sensation you can recognize as a warning sign, like a tight throat, sweaty palms, or a sinking feeling in your stomach. When you notice any of these signs of negative self-talk, pause to listen to the conversation. Write down what you hear your inner critic saying and keep a list.

2. *Take responsibility.* Once you have a catalog of your inner critic's greatest hits, be aware that you can choose to change the music. Just like with fear and resistance, you don't have to let these negative messages stop you. Begin by constructing a fair and accurate response to each of the messages you typically hear and use your response whenever you notice it. If your negative self-talk threatens, "They are going to say no to you," you might respond, "Yes, that's possible, but they also might say yes. I'll never know until I ask." If your inner critic tells you, "Don't do that—you might make a mistake," a good response is, "Yes, I might, but I'll learn from it and move on." Learning to manage negative self-talk is an attainable skill; the only requirement is that you be willing to try.

3. *Practice self-management.* Learning any new skill takes practice and managing your inner critic is no exception. At first it may be difficult to catch your inner critic in the act; you may realize only later where the reluctance you were feeling was coming from. This is a normal part of learning self-management. Just use your positive response as soon as you think of it. With practice, you will become more skilled at hearing negative messages in "real time," and be better able to respond immediately. If you use this process consistently, the messages will begin to lose their power over you because you will stop believing them.

Thought for the day: The main difference between a skill and a talent is a lot of practice.

DAY 16

Rest Day. Have fun today! Enjoy an activity you haven't done for a while to make the day feel special. You deserve it!

Thought for the day: Rule One in the Game of Life: You must be present to win.

DAY 17

Morning Review. It's the first working day of Week Three, and you're past the halfway mark in the program. Good work! Your target scores for each day this week should continue to be eight or higher on your Daily Actions, and 50 to 75 percent on your Success Ingredients. The focus this week will be on your Program Goal. At this point in the program you should have reached at least 50 percent of your goal. By the week's end, you will need to be at 75 percent. Ask yourself this morning, "What will it take to make this happen?"

Daily Scores. Did you see some movement toward your Program Goal today? If you are already at 75 percent or above, consider raising the stakes. How much more business could you generate by the end of next week? If you're below 50 percent, revisit your Daily Actions. Do you need to boost your level of effort in order to get more clients? Consider increasing the quantity or frequency of your Daily Actions to make up the gap between you and your goal. Make your weekly actions twice a week; double your target number for calls, letters, or meetings. You've only got two weeks left, so make the most of them.

Thought for the day:

> *If he who has a thing to sell*
> *Goes and whispers in a well,*

He won't be so apt to make the dollars
As he who climbs a tree and hollers!

—Anonymous

DAY 18

Morning Review. What can you do to ensure you're pulled toward your Program Goal rather than having to push to get there? Take a moment to reread the first section of your Action Worksheet from Chapter 3. How did you answer "What would that get you?" when you thought about the level of business you really want? Now visualize some of those results. Pick one to be your touchstone for the day and post a word, phrase, or picture somewhere to remind you of it: on your phone, computer, or dashboard.

   Daily Scores. Did you feel some pull from your goal today? Try creating an even stronger touchstone for yourself this evening with one of these quick activities:

   1. *Write about it.* Write down what it would be like to achieve your goal. What would you have? How would you feel? What could you then do?

   2. *Draw it.* Draw a picture of what goal achievement would look like. You don't have to be an artist; even stick figures drawn with markers will do the trick.

   3. *Visualize it.* Close your eyes, put on some soothing music, and create your detailed vision of success as you imagine it.

   4. *Sing it.* If there's a song that represents achievement or good fortune to you, play it and sing along. Or change the words to any song on the radio to be about you and your success.

   Thought for the day: When doing business with the universe, remember that you must place an order if you want to get a delivery.

DAY 19

Morning Review. Use the touchstone you created yesterday to help motivate you today. Post your essay or picture on the wall, recapture your visualization by briefly closing your eyes, or hum your success song.

   Daily Scores. Are you past the 50 percent mark toward your Program Goal? Yes? Keep it up! No? If you are still struggling, revisit "Choosing Where to Focus" in Chapter 2 where you selected the stage of the Universal Marketing Cycle you would work on this month. Do you think you chose correctly? Has anything changed or shifted since you made your choice? If you're not sure, look at the Daily Actions listed in Chapter 5 for the other stage or stages you are considering. Do any of those actions seem more appropriate for where you are now?

If you've been working at a high level of activity for the last two and a half weeks, it is entirely possible that you have moved forward a stage in the marketing cycle. It's also possible that by becoming more active about marketing, you have discovered that your challenges are not what you originally thought they were. If either of these situations exists for you, it's time to redo your Daily Actions list to better match where you are now.

Thought for the day: When you are selling professional services, the client's resistance is often about taking the action that your service represents, and not at all about hiring you. If you can get the client to commit to taking action on what needs to be done, hiring you will be his natural next step.

DAY 20

Morning Review. You have two days left to reach a 75 percent score on your Program Goal. What sort of game could you design for yourself to play that would make these two days exciting and fun? Could you see how many phone calls you could make in an hour or how many business cards you could collect at a single meeting? Is there a buddy with whom you could play this game and have the winner buy lunch?

Daily Scores. What was it like to be more playful with marketing today? Could you play the same game tomorrow or invent a different one? What could you reward yourself with this weekend if you get to 75 percent on your Program Goal by the end of Friday?

Thought for the day: Struggle and adventure are two sides of the same coin. When you find yourself struggling, flip it over.

DAY 21

Morning Review. Set yourself up for an exciting, adventurous day. Take some risks, put yourself out there, really go for it!

Daily Scores. It's the end of Week Three and you have been steadily in action about marketing for twenty-one days. You definitely deserve some applause. If you are at 75 percent or higher on your Program Goal, you are right on target. If you aren't quite there, congratulate yourself anyway on how much you have learned. We'll look tomorrow at whether you need to make any changes.

Thought for the day: Marketing is like a box of chocolates because (1) you never know what you're going to get; (2) nobody likes all of it; and (3) there are plenty of treats, but you have to look to find them.

DAY 22

Rest Day. So how did Week Three go? Does it look like you'll be able to reach 100 percent of your goal by the end of next week? It's time to revisit your goal one more time and see if it is serving you the way it should. Goals work differently for different people. Some folks like ambitious goals that they can't quite reach because it makes them try harder. Others find that this approach backfires because they always feel as if they're not doing enough; setting a goal that they know they can achieve is much more satisfying. Which type are you?

If ambitious goals excite you and make you want to get up in the morning, and your Program Goal is at 75 percent or more right now, raise it. Give yourself a reason to go all out in the final week. If on the other hand it's important to you that you reach every goal you set for yourself, and you're below 75 percent right now, lower your target. This is not cheating! If you can't win the game, there will be a piece of you that doesn't want to play anymore. By setting a more achievable goal, you will continue to be motivated by it.

Thought for the day: Goal setting works the same way as target practice. Without a target, you don't know what you're shooting at, and until you start shooting, you don't know how far off your aim is.

DAY 23

Rest Day. Did you promise yourself a reward for reaching your Program Goal target this week? Today is a good day to keep your promise. If you didn't make your target, what reward do you get for trying?

Thought for the day: Rest restores, repose repositions, recreation recreates.

DAY 24

Morning Review. You're on the home stretch with only five more days to go. Your target scores for each day this week should be eight or higher on your Daily Actions, and 75 to 100 percent on your Success Ingredients and your Program Goal. Picture the reward for achieving your Program Goal that you chose in Chapter 3. If you reach your goal by Friday, that prize will be yours!

The focus of Week Four is learning. As you have been working your way through the Get Clients Now! program, you have discovered some significant information about how you handle sales and marketing. If you can capture that learning and use it to become a better marketer, you will have accomplished an important result this month. Finding out that you never leave enough time for follow-up is just as valuable to your ultimate success as getting three new clients.

As you plan your day this morning and complete your Daily Actions throughout the day, notice:

- What have you learned about time management?
- Are you managing projects, priorities, and your schedule any differently than you did at the beginning of the program?
- What is working for you about the way you manage time?
- What still isn't working well?

Daily Scores. Were you able to balance all the program elements today: Success Ingredients, Daily Actions, Program Goal, and Special Permission? Take a few moments to write down what you have learned about time management over the last twenty-four days.

Thought for the day:
There once was a person named Lou
Who found he had too much to do.
So his very first task
Was learning to ask
Who to give Lou's to-do's to?

DAY 25

Morning Review. Have you designed a getting-clients game to play this week? Or is there some other way you can keep marketing light and fun? Humor and a sense of playfulness are effective antidotes to fear and resistance. Notice throughout today what you are learning about these two tough adversaries.

Daily Scores. Write down your thoughts about these questions:

- What have you learned about fear and resistance?
- When do they surface for you?
- What does their appearance signal?
- What strategies have worked for you in handling these saboteurs?
- Where do you still have trouble?

Thought for the day: When you are faced with an obstacle, imagine you are an inquisitive child at a locked gate. Depending on your skills and talents, you might climb over it, tunnel under it, go for help, pick the lock, or break down the fence. The one thing you wouldn't do is stand there wondering how it got locked in the first place.

DAY 26

Morning Review. Keep that reward visible; you're almost there! If you have been working with a business buddy, action group, or coach, is there any extra assistance you'd like to ask for in these last three days to help you meet your goal? Consider today what you have learned about support this month.

Daily Scores. As of today, your Program Goal should be at 90 percent or more. Ask yourself what you should do in the next two days to reach 100 percent. Then take a moment to focus on your learning about support:

- Is there any support you need to ask for now from your family, friends, or colleagues?
- What kind of support has been most helpful to you in the past month?
- Have you found yourself willing to ask for support, or do you wait until you are in a crisis?
- What support structures would be beneficial to maintain after you complete the program?

Thought for the day: Asking for help is not cheating. It's how anything important ever gets done.

DAY 27

Morning Review. Is there anything that will get in the way of your being successful today? Are you willing to set aside whatever comes up? Notice what you are learning about self-management.

Daily Scores. Only one more day to go. Take a deep breath, and smile big! Notice what you have learned about your inner critic during the program:

- What are the "greatest hits" playing on your negative self-talk jukebox?
- Are there some counter-messages you designed that work particularly well?
- How does your inner critic interfere with your ability to market?
- What changes have you noticed in your ability to manage this interference?

Thought for the day: If you don't like the music, don't dance to it.

DAY 28

Morning Review. Are you ready to win? Are you planning your victory celebration? Can you taste your reward? You have earned it! Think about the element of motivation today:

- What really motivates you?

- How did having a specific goal for the month change your behavior?

- Does a far-off goal draw you toward it or do you need to be getting more enjoyment in the moment?

- Do you reward yourself for progress and learning or only if you achieve certain results?

- Are you satisfied with rewarding yourself or do you want acknowledgment from others?

- What motivational techniques backfire on you? Which are your favorites?

Daily Scores. You did it! Way to go! If you reached 100 percent or more on your Program Goal, you have achieved complete success in the Get Clients Now! program. If your score is lower, you still deserve a huge commendation for sticking with the program. And you probably learned even more than those who did reach 100 percent.

What have you learned about goal-setting, about marketing, about selling? What did you learn if you didn't meet your goal? The fact is that marketing is just another skill that you learn by practicing over time, and you have had a lot of practice this month. If you have always tended to reward yourself only for results, try acknowledging your progress regardless of the outcome. You may find this shift in thinking beneficial in more areas than marketing!

Thought for the day: Success in marketing depends on success in management. The way you manage time, money, projects, people, and your own worst doubts and fears has as much to do with getting clients as advertising, publicity, and cold calling do. Always remember that what you are really selling is you, so developing yourself is the best marketing investment you can make.

What's Next for You?

Whew! You've just completed an intensive 28-day program to get more clients. After you celebrate and catch your breath, you will probably be wondering what's next. The Get Clients Now! program is designed to be used over and over. Next month, or whenever you feel the need for a marketing boost, you can design a new program for yourself and start again.

Whether you are repeating the program immediately or not, review now your notes about what you learned over the past month. Look again at each of the areas you examined in Week Four—time management, fear and resistance, support, self-management, and motivation. How can you develop your skills in these areas to become better at marketing? What will you do differently in the future based on what you learned throughout the program about goal-setting, marketing, and selling?

Look also at your chosen Success Ingredients. Are any of these projects still incomplete? What additional projects back in Chapter 4 did you consider choosing, and is now the time to move forward on any of these?

Save your notes about learning areas and Success Ingredients to help design your next Get Clients Now! program. When you are ready to start again, begin by rediagnosing your marketing condition with the Universal Marketing Cycle in Chapter 2.

If you went through the program by yourself this time, consider repeating it with a buddy, group, or coach to see how much difference the extra accountability, perspective, and support can make to your success. Or perhaps you see another way to make this program more effective for the way you think and work. Be creative, find your own unique solution, and above all, have fun!

Part III

The Strategies

Introduction to Part III

You may have reached Part III because you are reading this book from beginning to end before completing the exercises or starting the design of your own Get Clients Now! program. The information here about marketing strategies, "recipes," and missing ingredients can certainly be used in this way to generate ideas and inspiration at any time.

A better way to make use of this material, however, is to reference it while you are in the process of building or implementing your action plan, for example, while:

- Selecting your Success Ingredients (Chapter 4)
- Choosing from the Action Plan Menu (Chapter 5)
- Putting the system in action (Chapter 6)

This part of the book contains instructions for preparing your chosen Success Ingredients, as well as marketing recipes to help you apply the strategies specified in your action plan. A chapter for each stage of the Universal Marketing Cycle is provided so you can quickly locate the ingredients and recipes you need:

- Filling the Pipeline (Chapter 7)
- Following Up (Chapter 8)
- Getting Presentations (Chapter 9)
- Closing Sales (Chapter 10)

You need only look at the specific chapter that covers the stage you are working on. Each chapter begins with an overview of the stage and some of the basic Success Ingredients it requires, then gives recipes for how to apply each marketing strategy during that stage. Only those strategies suitable for the stage are included, usually in this order:

- Direct Contact and Follow-Up
- Networking and Referral-Building
- Public Speaking
- Writing and Publicity
- Promotional Events
- Advertising

You need only study those strategies you are actually planning to use. For each strategy, additional Success Ingredients specific to that strategy are described within the recipe that most closely relates to them. For example, the ingredient "prospect list" can be found under the recipe for "Calling and Mailing," and the ingredient "press release/media kit" is described in the recipe for "Getting Media Publicity." The Success Ingredients covered in each section are listed at the beginning so you can find them easily.

Happy cooking!

Chapter 7

Filling the Pipeline: When You Don't Know Enough People to Contact

"Our grand business is not to see what lies dimly at a distance, but to do what lies clearly at hand."

—Thomas Carlyle

Making Your Strategies Work

Filling your marketing pipeline with prospects, contacts, leads, and referrals will be an ongoing process for as long as you are in business. By choosing to focus on this stage of the marketing cycle now, you are acknowledging that this is the area of your marketing that currently needs the most effort. Later on, when you have overcome some of your pipeline-filling challenges, you may decide to focus more energy on one of the other stages. But it is important to recognize that you will always need to keep your pipeline full.

This means that whatever marketing strategies you decide on for filling the pipeline, you should be willing to keep them up over an extended period of time. In marketing, more of the same works much better than a little of everything. Ideally, your pipeline-filling activities should become automatic and habitual. Even when you are busy, you should always allow time for making new contacts, networking, speaking, or whatever your chosen strategies are.

It's natural to wonder whether the strategies you have selected are the best choices. You may find yourself wanting to switch around just to see if something else might work better. Be patient and don't change your pipeline-filling strategies during the twenty-eight days of the Get Clients

Now! program. It simply isn't enough time for you to judge your results accurately. It's okay to change individual *tactics;* you might switch from cold calling to warm calling, for example. But don't alter your overall *strategies*, from say networking and referral building to promotional events.

The best way to determine how well a particular strategy is working to fill your pipeline is to track your results over time. There are three statistics that will be helpful to you in evaluating the strategies you are using:

1. How many prospects did each strategy generate?

2. How many sales resulted from those prospects?

3. What was the dollar value of those sales?

If you carefully note the exact source of each prospect, you can easily track these statistics for the month of the program. If you keep tracking your results for three months, six months, or a year, you will have a much more accurate perspective on which marketing strategies work best. Then if you decide to make a change, choose just one new strategy at a time to try out. And remember to keep tracking.

Who Belongs in Your Pipeline

There are two broad categories of people and organizations you want in your marketing pipeline: those who may someday be clients, and those who can refer clients. To find people who are likely to become clients, you will want to reach out to a market niche that is a good match for your service. To find people who may never be clients but could refer you business, reach out to those who serve or interact with people in that niche.

A person or group who doesn't fall into one of these two categories probably doesn't belong in your pipeline. It is true that people you meet in the course of doing business may become personal friends or helpful resources, but you don't want to use up your precious marketing time in following up with folks who are neither likely to be clients nor refer them.

Whenever you meet someone outside your market niche who also doesn't seem to have much contact with it, think twice before putting that person in your pipeline. Always concentrate your efforts on the most likely prospects and referral partners. The way to win the marketing game is not to collect the most names and phone numbers, but to make the most sales.

Ingredients for Filling the Pipeline

Success Ingredients

Description of services

Market niche definition

10-second introduction

Business cards

Website

INGREDIENT: *Description of Services*

Being able to describe clearly the services you offer is essential for all aspects of marketing. A solid **description of services** can be the basis of numerous other marketing tools, such as a brochure, website, or telephone script. A complete description contains the features, benefits, structure, and cost of your services. The example in Figure 7-1 is for a certified public accountant serving small business owners.

Figure 7-1 Description of Services Example

I provide tax preparation services for income, payroll, sales, and other miscellaneous taxes. I advise my clients on tax compliance and how to minimize their taxes. I also prepare business and personal financial statements. Other services I offer are analyzing employee benefit and retirement packages, valuing the worth of a business, and advice on accounting and financial software packages.

Benefits of using my service include saving money on taxes, complying with government regulations to avoid penalties, having accurate information to manage your business at your fingertips, and letting someone else worry about keeping up with tax laws so you don't have to.

I charge for my services on an hourly basis, at $100 per hour.

INGREDIENT: *Market Niche Definition*

Your **market niche definition** identifies the group of people, organizations, and issues that your business is primarily designed to serve. These are the prospects you plan to pursue actively as clients. Don't make the mistake of thinking that your niche definition must encompass everyone who could possibly be a client. Instead, decide which clients you truly want.

Choosing and defining a specific niche allows you to maximize all of your marketing efforts. Without a niche, your marketing attempts will be diluted and haphazard, leading to wasted effort, muddy marketing messages, and an overwhelming number of choices about where to go, who to contact, and what to say. Making a name for yourself as a professional will be almost impossible because prospects won't be able to distinguish your true expertise.

The most powerful niche definitions include both a target market and a specialty. Your target market is the audience your business serves, and your specialty is the scope of issues you address with your clients—the goals you help them achieve and the problems you assist them to solve. For example, a real estate agent's niche might be "South Houston buyers of income property." If this seems too narrow a definition to you, consider the alternative. A broad description like "Gulf Coast buyers of real estate" will attract no one. It's far too generic to be useful in crafting marketing messages or focusing your marketing action plan.

Here are some questions to help you identify your market niche:

- Who needs your service the most?
- Who is able to pay what you need to charge?
- Who is likely to give you large orders or repeat business?
- Whose problems and goals do you care about?
- What type of client work provides you with the most enjoyment and satisfaction?
- What sort of people do you enjoy spending time with?
- Where do you already have many contacts or an established reputation?
- Who would be the easiest clients to get?

Remember that what you are doing here is targeting a particular group, not excluding all others. You are not limiting your options by choosing a market niche; instead you are organizing yourself to launch an effective marketing campaign aimed at the clients you most want. If someone outside that niche shows up in your pipeline, by all means do business with them if you like. But focus your outgoing efforts on filling the pipeline with those clients you are most interested in getting.

For the target market portion of your niche definition, it's important to describe your market using demographics or industry classifications, rather than the presumed need of a client for your service. A contract trainer specializing in conflict resolution skills, for example, would find little value in defining her target market as "organizations that experience conflict." This could be anyone.

"Organizations in need of conflict resolution training" won't do the job as a definition either. Could you look them up in a directory? Would a referral partner know who would be a good lead for you? Could you figure out where these people would go to network? No. You can't do any of these things with a need-based definition.

But if the trainer defined her market as "human resource development or training managers in midsize to large companies located in the Boston area," now she can find them—and so can her referral partners.

If your target market is organizations, here are some ways you could define them:

Classification (e.g., retailer, manufacturer, government agency)

Industry (e.g., health care, software, travel)

Size (by number of employees or annual revenue)

Geographical Location

Special Characteristics (e.g., well-established, rapidly growing, family friendly)

Decision Makers (by department, division, or position title)

And here are some ways to define individuals as prospective clients:

Age

Gender

Family Status (e.g., married, children, aging parents)

Occupation (e.g., student, executive, self-employed professional)

Income (by individual or household)

Education (e.g., high school, college, post-graduate)

Geographical Location

Interests and Hobbies (e.g., sports enthusiast, active investor, entertains often)

For the specialty segment of your niche definition, choose words or phrases that your target audience would typically use themselves when describing the problems or goals they need assistance with. People seeking interior design help might have goals such as "furnish a new home," "remodel the kitchen," or "stage the house for sale." You could echo these needs by labeling your specialty as "custom home furnishings," "kitchen and bath remodeling," or "home staging." Stay away from generic, abstract phrases like "innovative designs" and "outstanding interiors." These may be useful in writing marketing copy for a brochure or website, but are inadequate as definitions of who you serve and how.

Join your target market and specialty together in one concise phrase that identifies your most-wanted target group and the problems or goals you address for them. For example: "network installation for small to midsize companies in the Denver area" or "career transition for midlife women."

A final word of advice: if you can't seem to narrow your focus to just one target market and specialty, you are better off defining two or three distinct markets or specialty areas than using one broad label intended to include them all in your niche definition. A financial planner seeking high-income individuals, for example, might choose "executives, established professionals, and successful entrepreneurs" as targeted groups. A target like this is much more helpful in locating prospects than saying "people with income over $100K."

INGREDIENT: *10-Second Introduction*

Your **10-second introduction** is a concise summary of your business that you can use when you shake someone's hand, stand up in front of a group, or make a sales presentation. It describes what you do and who you do it for in a clear and memorable way. One effective format is the benefits-oriented introduction, where you state the key benefit of your service before giving your occupation or job title. Here are some examples:

> "My name is Joyce Ozier and I help Vancouver retailers get more window shoppers into their stores. My company is Wow! Windows, and we provide retail display and design."

"My name is Peter Marconi and I provide Chicago financial services firms with persuasive tools for winning new clients. I'm a marketing communications consultant."

"I'm Carrie Greene, and I help people with Attention Deficit Disorder gain control of their lives and carry through with their goals. The name of my company is CarrieThru. I'm a personal coach and professional organizer."

"I'm Fred Patel, and I deliver talented, high-caliber professionals to fill essential positions at information technology companies nationwide. I'm an executive recruiter."

The advantage of this format is that it positions you in the mind of the listeners before they have a chance to form their own opinions about what you do. If you introduce yourself as an attorney, for example, your listener may think you are a litigator, estate planner, or do criminal defense work, none of which helps you get clients if you do family law. An introduction that begins, "I work with people going through divorce to help them get what they're entitled to," is both more specific and more memorable.

Notice that all these introductions use plain language rather than industry jargon. Unless you know exactly who your listeners are and what vernacular they speak, use terms a 12-year-old would understand.

INGREDIENT: *Business Cards*

The main purpose of a **business card** is to facilitate communication, not to give a complete description of your services. Put just enough information on your card for people to remember what you do, but not so much that they have no reason to call you or visit your website. If you turn your business card into a brochure, people won't contact you to learn more, nor will you have anything additional to provide them with after you meet.

Include your name, company name if you have one, mailing address, phone, fax, e-mail address, and website, if applicable. If you are operating a home business and prefer to keep your address confidential, provide at least your city and state. If your company name makes it clear what you do, that may be all you need. Otherwise, choose from just one of the following ways to indicate your profession:

1. *Title or Function* (e.g., graphic designer, event planning, business broker).

2. *Specialties*. List no more than three (e.g., employment law—employee relations—dispute resolution; errands—organizing—filing; psychotherapy—consultation—training).

3. *Tag Line* (e.g., "Strategic research in values and attitudes," "Helping nonprofits thrive," "Stress relief for overworked professionals").

If you want to add more value to your card, instead of cataloging the features and benefits of your service, include a sample of your expertise or an invitation to take the next step. For example, a chiropractor might include the line "Call for a free initial consultation on pain relief," or a career counselor could print a brief "career satisfaction quiz" on the back of her card.

The more expensive your service is, the more expensive your card should look. Adding color, a logo, or your photograph, using embossing, or choosing high-quality paper are all ways of improving the look of your card. You may need the services of a professional graphic designer to boost the image your card projects. If you will be relying on mailed information to impress prospective clients, your card will need to match the design of your letterhead, brochure, or marketing kit. Avoid using perforated card stock to print cards from your own computer. Cards like these give the impression that you aren't willing to invest in your business and won't inspire trust.

When you are marketing more than one business, you need more than one business card. Even if you find yourself giving both cards to the same person, they will represent what you offer much more clearly than if you try to put everything on the same card.

INGREDIENT: *Website*

A **website** can be a powerful tool for filling the pipeline, following up, or both. Many professional services sites are primarily online brochures. Their content focuses on describing the features and benefits of the services being offered and provides supporting details such as biographies or client lists. If your website matches this description, you will probably find that your site is primarily a follow-up tool. Most of your site visitors will not find you on their own, but will instead be people you direct to your site by way of other pipeline-filling strategies such as direct contact, public speaking, writing, or advertising. The elements of a basic website like this typically include:

- Description of the services you offer
- Details about your target market or professional specialty (e.g., "I work with artists and designers" or "We specialize in qualitative market research")
- Features and benefits of your services
- Tag line, positioning statement, or competitive advantage
- Biography of you, your company, or both
- Client list, testimonials, or endorsement quotes
- Photographs or illustrations of you or your work
- Contact information: address, phone, fax, and e-mail

There's nothing wrong with having a website that follows this online brochure model. For many professionals, this may be all the Web presence you need. However, if you wish to use your site not just to follow up with prospects but also to fill the pipeline by attracting new visitors—without paid advertising—you will need more. To accomplish this aim, you will need to build a site that offers more value beyond just marketing copy, and employs search engine positioning techniques to draw traffic.

Adding fresh, informative content to your site increases its value as a resource, which will bring you a higher ranking in the search engines, build your professional credibility, encourage other sites to link to yours, and cause more people to refer others to your site. These added information pages will also provide multiple links to your site in the search engines, because each one will be indexed separately. Posting new content frequently will also improve your search engine ranking. Adding value to your site can take the form of:

- Educational articles about your area of expertise
- Quizzes or assessments your visitors can use to score themselves
- Frequently Asked Questions (FAQs) about your field
- Resource directories or links to other useful sites
- White papers, case studies, or surveys relevant to your industry
- Tutorials or how-to guides that showcase your specialty

Search engine positioning techniques can improve the ranking of your site in search engine results when prospects search for specific keywords or keyword phrases. The higher your site ranks in the results, the more likely it is that a searcher will visit. If you can identify what search terms your best prospects are most likely to use, you can feature these terms prominently in your website's copy and in the hidden "metatags" used to code your site. The best terms to focus on are those directly relevant to what you offer, but not so highly competitive that getting a high rank will be difficult. Here's an example:

> A massage therapist in Tampa, Florida, found that typing "Tampa massage" into Google returned 1,900,000 results. Instead of trying to get a high ranking under that keyword phrase, she chose "Tampa deep tissue massage" for which there were only 78,000 results. In designing her site, she used the keyword phrase "Tampa deep tissue massage" in the page title on her home page, and in the keyword and description metatags hidden in the page's code. In the text on her page, she used the heading "deep tissue massage" when describing her work, and made sure to include that phrase and the word "Tampa" twice more in subsequent paragraphs. As a result, when her home page was indexed by Google, her site was listed in the top ten under "Tampa deep tissue massage." If she had resisted naming a specialty and focused her site around the more competitive phrase "Tampa massage" instead, it's unlikely she could have achieved a rank high enough for prospects to find her through a Google search.

Search engine positioning is a sophisticated tactic and you may not wish to spend time learning enough to use it on your own. Search engine optimization experts and some (but not all) Web designers can provide you with professional help.

Regarding design and construction of your site, hiring a Web designer will save you a great deal of frustration and produce a higher quality result than you are likely to produce on your own. Be sure to ask about the range of the designer's knowledge. If you are working with someone whose skills are mainly artistic or primarily technical, you may want to also hire a marketing pro to help with copywriting or search engine optimization.

Before you start building a site, spend some time surfing. Search for keywords you think prospective clients would use to find you, and explore what your competitors' sites contain. Make a list of features you like and dislike, as well as what you think the competitive advantages featured on your site should be.

Climbing to the Top of Mt. Search Engine

Jill Whalen is a search engine optimization expert and publishes the newsletter *High Rankings® Advisor*. Jill advises, "Top level search engine listings are absolutely critical for the success of your business on the Web. Why? According to most studies, the average user never goes past the third page of search results.

"Be realistic about your keyword choices. Never expect a high ranking for a single word—there are simply too many sites on the Internet for a one-word search to be effective. In addition, it's practically impossible to create a one-word search that is targeted to your specific website.

"For example, suppose you sell real estate in Florida. You might assume that using 'homes' as your keyword would produce a lot of targeted traffic. Wrong. Just because people search for the word 'homes' doesn't mean they're looking to buy or sell a home in Florida. However, if you choose 'moving to Florida' as your keywords, most of your site visitors will be people actually interested in moving to Florida, and therefore probably needing real estate. This is the beauty of choosing the proper keyword phrases: you get an extremely targeted audience!

"Once you do have relevant keyword phrases chosen for your site, you absolutely *must* write good, professional, keyword-rich marketing copy (or hire someone to do so) on every page of your website. You almost don't have to do anything else other than have some links pointing to it and you will rank high.

"It's important to note that simply being found in the engines isn't always enough. Once found, your site still has to sell its products or services. I believe that a big reason why our optimized sites end up getting so much new business is because we increase their overall appeal. That is, we write great, professional marketing text, and suggest other changes that may give the site a more professional appearance. These things are just as important to the bottom line as getting a high ranking in the first place."

Jill Whalen
www.highrankings.com

There are many ways to attract traffic to your website beyond those discussed above, and you'll find additional suggestions in this chapter under the recipes given for individual marketing strategies. Whichever methods you choose, however, beware of spending more time and money on building a site and attracting traffic to it than those visitors will ultimately be worth to you. In most cases, you will still need to have personal contact with prospects who find you on the Web before they decide to hire you. A well-designed website can be a significant source of new leads as well as a credibility booster, but it's not a complete sales and marketing strategy all by itself.

 Strategy: Direct Contact and Follow-Up

> ### Success Ingredients
>
> Prospect list
>
> Lead sources

RECIPE: *Calling and Mailing*

Sending mail or e-mail and placing calls are activities more typical of the following up stage than when filling the pipeline. This makes sense when you think about the whole purpose of your pipeline-filling activities: to find people you can call or mail, or to get people to contact you. So if you are working on filling the pipeline, you may not have a list of people to contact.

But there are two situations where you may wish to call and mail to help get your pipeline full: contacting new people to see if they might become prospects (more common in business-to-business marketing than when marketing to consumers), and contacting people you already know to stimulate referrals. You'll find information about both of these subjects in Chapter 8 also.

Whenever you contact someone new, the best approach is to call before you mail or e-mail them, and call again after you mail. Even if you don't reach the person on the first call, you can find out more information from his or her voice mail or the receptionist, and leave a message to expect an e-mail or letter from you. On your post-mailing call, if you again don't reach him, you can mention your letter or e-mail, and prompt him to read it if he hasn't yet.

The purpose of your calls is twofold: to find out if this lead is actually a good prospect for you, and if so, to try to make a presentation. Remember that a presentation is simply the time when you tell your prospects what you can do for them. It's not necessarily anything formal, and may happen on the phone instead of in person.

To accomplish your objectives, you will need to ask questions, not just give information. When you reach your prospect on the phone, don't rattle off a long introduction. Instead, give your name and mention any connection between you; then move immediately into conversation by asking a question. "Do you have a moment to talk about how I can help your company get better results from its training programs?" is a sample opening.

Be ready with two or three questions that will tell you immediately whether the person you are speaking with has a need for your service. If the need is there, ask for a meeting on the spot, or if you normally present by phone, do it right then. Don't back away by offering to send literature first or referring your prospect to your website. You may never get this person live on the phone again. Only if he declines to meet with you or to take time for your phone presentation should you offer to send something or suggest he visit your site. This is also a polite way to end the conversation if the answers to your qualifying questions indicate this is not a prospect for you.

The people you might be calling if you are trying to fill the pipeline are likely to be those you looked up on a **prospect list** you purchased or compiled from a directory or the Web, or obtained from a **lead source**, such as the media or a networking pal. (See "Finding Prospects" below for more information.) The best kind of mail to send folks like this is a personal letter or e-mail. "Personal" means addressed to them by name and mentioning some situation that you have reason to believe exists and that you can help with. If you are using postal mail, you can enclose a brochure or fact sheet, but don't send a lot of material. Wait for the follow-up stage to send anything more. And absolutely do follow up.

There's no hard and fast rule about whether postal mail or e-mail is a better choice for a cold contact like this. Sometimes an e-mail will get through to a prospect while a letter might be discarded by a gatekeeper. On the other hand, many people simply delete all e-mail from people they don't know. If you are using the call-mail-call sequence, your first call will alert your prospect to look for your e-mail, so he will be less likely to mistake it for an anonymous message sent to thousands of recipients. But with some prospects, only a postal letter will get their attention. You may wish to try both approaches.

When contacting people you already know in order to fill the pipeline, you are hoping to encourage referrals by reminding them who you are and what you do. Those you contact might be former clients, people you have presented to in the past who didn't buy, or networking contacts.

You might choose to get in touch with these people by phone, and place a "what's new" call. With centers of influence or likely referral partners, you might wish to schedule coffee or lunch. An easy way to contact a larger number of people, though, is by mail or e-mail. Again, personal mailings can have more impact than mass mailings of postcards or newsletters. An article, event announcement, or link to a useful website with a simple "thought you would be interested" note is a friendly and effective variety of reminder.

RECIPE: *Meeting People in Person*

Getting out of your office to meet people in person can be a welcome break from calling and mailing. (There's lots more information about this under the "Networking and Referral Building" strategy below.) Keep in mind, though, that you don't have to go to an official networking event to meet people. You meet new people all the time—at the grocery store, dentist's office, or your child's soccer game. Do all these people know what you do for a living?

Get in the habit of carrying your business cards everywhere. Whenever you meet someone, use your 10-second introduction, offer a business card, and ask for the other person's if they have one. You may feel awkward about this at first, but if you keep it up, it will soon become natural. If your service is primarily marketed to consumers rather than businesses—wedding planning, chiropractic, or home organizing, for example—this informal way of meeting new prospects can be quite fruitful.

And don't rule out this tactic if you market to organizations. All organizations are run by human beings, after all. That guy on the jogging path may turn out to be the marketing director of your city's fastest-growing firm, and the woman ahead of you in the espresso line might be the chief financial officer of a Fortune 500 corporation.

RECIPE: *Finding Prospects*

The best way to find prospects is by using the pipeline-filling strategies of networking and referral building, public speaking, and writing and publicity, described later in this chapter. This is because these approaches provide you with increased credibility, perceived endorsements, and personal connections, all of which build the know, like, and trust factor that makes people buy. But you can also locate prospective clients through research techniques if you have done a good job of defining your target market.

If you need a large number of prospects, you can license a targeted **prospect list** from a professional list broker or an online vendor of business lists or consumer lists (search the Web for "prospect lists" or "sales leads"). A compiled list like this can be useful if you are sending out direct mail to invite people to a seminar, or hiring a telemarketer to pitch free initial consultations for a professional services business with several principals. But for a solo professional doing a call-mail-call campaign, licensing a compiled list may give you more names than you can possibly use during the term of your license.

For smaller numbers, especially when marketing to businesses, it may make more sense to compile your own list. Some source data can be purchased in digital form, or, for infrequent use, you can find print sources in your local library. Here are some sources for compiling prospect lists:

- Internet searches for your target market and geographical area (e.g., "Portland hospitals," "Atlanta restaurants")

- Online business and industry directories (e.g., Hoover's, Thomas Register)

- Company directories (e.g., Dun and Bradstreet, Standard and Poor's)

- Yellow Pages and other advertising directories

- Trade directories (e.g., Chamber of Commerce, Better Business Bureau)

- Association membership rosters (online and in print)

- Leading company lists (e.g., those published by *Forbes* or *Fortune*)

- *Book of Lists* published by your local *Business Times* or *Business Journal*

- Tenant directory posted in the lobby of an office building or industrial park

When compiling a list of individuals you plan to call at their home phone numbers, be aware that for U.S. residents, the Federal Trade Commission's telemarketing regulations prohibit making sales calls to people with whom you have no prior relationship if their number is listed in the National Do Not Call Registry. While the FTC doesn't typically enforce these rules against individuals and small businesses who

Get a List and Get Going

"There's a lot of information available for free," points out list broker Lisa Bowen, "but you have to consider the cost of using it, too. Making photocopies at the library or entering names into your computer one by one from a directory gets old pretty quick. You can get an already-compiled list for less than you think. Work with a full-service list broker like me if you're interested in licensing 5,000 names or more. Or for smaller lists, you can deal with online services like AccuLeads or Dun and Bradstreet's Zapdata. You can get a list already on disk or download the data and put it into your contact management system. This is absolutely worth it in terms of productivity. Instead of working on compiling the list, you can get on the phone.

"It's easy to find a list of companies that fit your profile, but one thing you really can't get is the names of all the marketing directors or all the human resource directors. You have to call up and ask, "Who is the person responsible for . . . ?" If you can't find a list that's exactly what you need, buy the closest match. It's much easier than compiling a list from scratch.

"Keep in mind the difference between prospects and suspects. Prospects are people you have talked to, so you and they both know they need your services. Suspects are people you think need you, but *they* don't know it yet. When you buy a list, you are getting suspects. To turn them into prospects, you have to make the calls.

"The names on business lists turn over about 40 percent a year, so don't get more names than you can use in a calendar quarter. Frequently when you call someone, you find out they've moved on. But you do get a good list of companies. The ideal thing would be to get to the point where you already know all the companies in your area and you just update the names."

Lisa Bowen
www.prospectstogo.com

make a low volume of sales calls, it's still a good idea to check these numbers against the Registry first, which you can do for free at the FTC's Do Not Call website. Business-to-business marketing is exempt from these regulations.

You can also develop your own ongoing **lead sources**, which might be professional or trade associations; educational institutions; print, broadcast, or Web media; online forums; or personal networking buddies. Associations and schools produce publications and events that will keep you in touch with what's happening in the industry or specialty they focus on. Print, broadcast, and Web media, and online forums like message boards, e-mail discussion groups, and social networking sites can do the same. The more targeted the periodical, program, or forum is to the market niche that interests you, the better.

The people who are speaking at these events, writing articles, participating online, and being interviewed, are all potential leads for you. Make note of any names or affiliations you learn from these sources. Finding out how to contact the person afterward is often the easy part.

A Word About Fear

It is completely normal to feel apprehensive about calling strangers on the phone. You have no idea how your call is going to be received, and if the person on the other end refuses to speak with you or isn't interested, it's hard not to take it personally. You may not even realize that you are afraid of making cold calls, but somehow, mysteriously, a hot lead will sit on your desk day after day and you just won't get around to picking up the phone. Perhaps you'll resort to sending a letter or e-mail without a companion phone call, which is nowhere near as effective.

Try asking yourself, "What is the worst thing that could possibly happen if I made that call?" Would it be hearing, "Don't bother me," or "Not interested"? Or would it be worse if the person you called was interested and you got tongue-tied and lost the sale? You know, though, if you don't place the call, you've lost the sale anyway. So how bad could making the call really be?

The fact is that most people are polite in their refusals. They say, "No, thank you," and hang up. And when someone is interested in what you have to offer, the conversation gets easy pretty quickly; your prospect may actually help you along.

What You Miss When You Fear to Persist

"The most common fright of all, perhaps, is that of rejection," muses Alan Weiss, author of 25 books, including the bestseller *Million Dollar Consulting* (McGraw-Hill, 2002). In his newsletter *The Balancing Act®*, Alan says, "We simply don't want to be unliked, unaccepted, or unappealing. I've seen people with superb credentials and qualifications surrender to the less well-informed and educated because they don't want to incur displeasure. In normal negotiations, whether over salary, assignments, or opportunities, many people refuse to support their own legitimate positions because they are frightened of being rejected or seen as resistant. The inevitable results of such acquiescence is that people become angry at themselves later for missing the moment, and engage in the debilitating rituals of 'I should have said. . . .' and 'Why didn't I. . . .' In other words, not only do they abandon the negotiation, but they beat themselves up later for doing so.

"We're frightened because our egos are involved. Our carefully sculpted self-identities might suffer if we are unattractive to others, not accepted by our peers, and not compliant with everyone's needs. Ironically, in being so afraid to alienate others, we end up alienating ourselves. We sacrifice our potential to help others by delimiting our own growth and goals. My son used to tell me that he wasn't frightened by the dark, he was frightened by what might be in the dark. Fair enough. Buy a flashlight and shine it on the worst rejection you can anticipate. You'll find there's little to worry about except your ego, and then you can stop being so frightened."

Alan Weiss, Ph.D.
www.summitconsulting.com

So what do you think: Can you pick up the phone? You'll never know what you are missing out on unless you make the call.

 **Strategy: Networking and Referral Building**

Success Ingredients

Networking venues

Referral partners

Networking skills

RECIPE: *Attending Events*

Meeting people at organized events is one of the easiest and most effective ways to fill your marketing pipeline—easy, that is, if you're not afraid of talking to strangers. All you have to do is match your market niche definition with the member profile of an existing association, organization, institution, or social group, and go shake hands.

The places where you go to meet people are your **networking venues**. Here are some popular choices for networking in person:

- Chamber of Commerce mixers, workshops, and award ceremonies
- Service clubs such as Rotary, Lions, and Kiwanis
- Trade and professional association meetings where your *clients* are likely to gather
- Trade and professional association meetings where your *referral partners* are likely to gather
- Lectures, classes, workshops, and conferences hosted by educational institutions, vendors, community organizations, and affinity groups
- Social, cultural, and sporting events or fund raisers that include receptions or other mix-and-mingle time
- Private gatherings organized for the purpose of meeting new people and schmoozing
- Lead exchange groups, where people in noncompetitive businesses gather weekly or monthly to swap leads and referrals

The best venues for networking are those intended to be a place for people to meet. If you attend a function like this, you can be assured that saying hello to someone you don't know will be accepted and welcome. Just walk up to anyone who looks interesting, stick out your hand, and say, "Hi, I haven't met you yet." Give the person your 10-second introduction and ask what he or she does.

If you are naturally shy, you may find that groups with a more structured format work better for you than informal mixers and receptions. Many networking events offer "introductions," which means that members get a chance to stand up and tell the whole group what they do. Attendees may also be able to display or distribute flyers, brochures, or business cards. Even more structured than this is a lead exchange group.

Where do you find groups and events like this? Start by asking around. Anyone who is a likely **referral partner** for you can probably suggest some. Here are some other places you can look:

- *Websites That List Events*. Do a keyword search for your city, e.g., "Boston events"

- *Yellow Pages*. Look under "Associations" or "Professional Organizations."

- *Regional and Local Newspapers*. Look for a "Business Calendar" or "Community Calendar" section.

- *Chamber of Commerce*. Ask for a list of local business and community organizations.

- *Business Times* or *Business Journal* for your metropolitan area.

- *Specialized Publications* aimed at your market niche's profession or area of special interest.

In looking for events to attend, keep in mind that the way to get the most value from a group is to be a member of it. You will have more success in your networking if you go back to the same groups over and over than if you keep going to new groups all the time. Find two or three that seem to have the right mix of people, and keep going back.

So what if you are uncomfortable talking to strangers? Acquiring good **networking skills** will benefit you in all areas of your marketing. It's important to learn to introduce yourself smoothly, start a conversation with someone you don't know, and be comfortable when talking about your business in social settings. You might try practicing with friends, look for a workshop you could take, or read one of the many books on networking or mingling.

RECIPE: *Following Up with Contacts*

If you don't follow up with the people you meet, you are wasting your time in meeting them. It is simply untrue that someone will "call you when they need you." The truth is that if they have met you only once, they probably don't even remember you, and it's even less likely that they will remember where they put your card.

In networking, remembering the know, like, and trust factor is critical. If you give people a chance to know you better, they will be much more likely to do business with you or refer others. But building relationships like this takes repeated contacts over time. There is much more about follow-up in Chapter 8, but the focus here is on how to follow up immediately with the people you meet at an event.

Take all those business cards out of your pocket and sort them into three piles: prospective clients, useful networking contacts, and other. Now sort the client pile into hot, warm, and cool leads. A hot lead would be someone who already expressed an interest in doing business with you. A warm lead would be someone who mentioned a problem or goal you know you can help with.

Stop right there and follow up with all the hot and warm leads. Call each one on the phone, reintroduce yourself, and try to make a presentation or get an appointment for one. If directly soliciting business is inappropriate due to your profession (psychotherapy, for example) or the nature of the relationship (perhaps you met at church), you can still make contact, perhaps with a "nice-to-meet-you" note. When you get voice mail or someone requests more information, send a letter or e-mail with a fact sheet or link to your website. Put the person on your calendar for the next follow-up.

Next, go to the useful networking contacts and sort them into two piles: people who you believe can lead you directly to prospective clients and people who can lead you to other marketing opportunities, such as a new networking group or a speaking engagement. Stop and follow up with the people who might ultimately have leads for you. Call them to suggest coffee or lunch, or offer to stop by the office. Remember your intention to build an ongoing relationship. Listen for clues about their interests, concerns, and goals. Consider what you might be able to offer them to create some reciprocity in your relationship.

You should now have three stacks of cards left: cool client leads, people who can lead you to marketing opportunities, and other. If you are short on time or have other hot leads in the pipeline, send those cool leads a nice-to-meet-you note, and tuck them away in your contact management system in case you need them later. If the new marketing opportunities fit into your current plans, go ahead and contact those people. Otherwise treat them just like the cool leads.

And those "other" cards? Unless they belong to people you would like to have a personal friendship with, throw them away. If they aren't worth following up with now, they don't belong in your contact management system.

RECIPE: *Networking with Referral Partners*

A **referral partner** is a person, group, or institution willing to refer potential clients to you. Building relationships with referral partners can be an almost effortless way to fill your marketing pipeline. If enough people begin referring business to you, you will eventually achieve the enviable position of being able to respond to client inquiries instead of having to initiate contact yourself.

A prospective client who is referred to you is much more likely to buy what you have to sell than someone who hasn't been referred. The endorsement of the person making the referral carries a lot of weight, increasing the know, like, and trust factor immediately. Referred prospects are less likely to shop for the lowest price, ask fewer questions about your background and expertise, and typically come to a decision much more quickly. If soliciting business is inappropriate in your profession, referrals may be your primary source of clients.

For all these reasons, concentrating effort on building referrals can be a very worthwhile use of your time. While some of the best referrals come from past clients, there are many other possible referral partners for any business. Here are some examples:

- *Other Prospects.* People you have spoken or met with but aren't ready to buy from you now will still refer you to others, if you remember to keep in touch with them.

- *Colleagues.* Others in your field can be excellent referral sources. If you offer noncompetitive services, you may even decide to collaborate on projects or approach prospective clients together.

- *Competitors.* Don't rule out your competitors as referral partners. You may have an area of specialty that they don't. They may also have times when they can't handle all the business that comes to them or can't take on a particular client because of a conflict of interest.

- *Others Who Serve Your Market.* Anyone who is in regular contact with your market niche is a potential referral partner, regardless of the field he or she is in. A computer network installer might easily collect referrals from the owner of a moving company, a commercial property manager, or a security systems salesperson—all people who might know about an upcoming office relocation. A strategic alliance with a partner like this could also allow you to bundle your services or products together.

• *Salespeople.* Regardless of what they sell, salespeople are used to the process of giving and receiving referrals. If you make friends with someone who sells for a living, he or she will naturally be on the lookout for possible leads for you. Start with the salespeople who sell to you.

• *Centers of Influence.* These are the people everyone seems to know. You see them at networking events, read their names in the trade press, and hear them mentioned everywhere. People like this get asked for referrals all the time, so you want your name to be in their contact management system.

• *Organizations.* When a prestigious nonprofit or educational institution refers you, it is an implied endorsement, and makes you very attractive to prospective clients. Building relationships with organizations like this typically requires volunteering your professional services or teaching for them.

To begin identifying potential referral partners, develop a list of categories that represents the type of people or groups you think would be good candidates. For example, if you were an executive recruiter specializing in start-ups and rapidly growing small companies, your referral partner categories might be:

- Accountants who serve this market
- Attorneys specializing in stock offerings, contracts, patents, trademarks, and other relevant areas
- Business development consultants
- Business and investment bankers
- Entrepreneurship centers
- Human resource management consultants
- Marketing consultants
- Venture capitalists

When you have identified some promising categories, look through your existing contacts to see who you already know that fits. Call those

Reframing Can Lead to Referring

"Referrals are the direct result of doing the correct things in the referral-gathering process," declares Bob Burg, author of *Endless Referrals* (McGraw-Hill, 2005). "Most people ask, 'Do you know anyone who would be a good prospect for my widgets?' This approach usually elicits a couple of seconds of deep thought followed by, 'Well, I can't think of anyone right now, but when I do, I'll call you.' Ah, but how often do they ever actually call?

"The problem is you're asking them to pick individuals out of a crowd in their mind of about 250 people. That's the average person's sphere of influence. It's like being asked if you've heard any good jokes lately. Personally, although I'm exposed to jokes every day over the Internet, I can never think of one at the time I'm asked.

"Tom Hopkins, in his book *How to Master the Art of Selling,* advises helping your referrer isolate specific people they can identify and remember by narrowing their frame of reference. How? Here's a brief example:

"You: Dave, you're an avid golfer, aren't you?

"Dave: Yes, I am. I play every weekend.

"You: Hmm. Is there a specific foursome you play with?

"Dave: Absolutely, Tom Smith, Rita Jones, and Harry Browne.

"You: Dave, would any of them seem to be good candidates for . . . ?

"One more example. We know Dave is a Rotarian. Instead of asking if "anyone" in Rotary would be a good prospect (that's still too large a frame), try:

"You: Are there one or two people in your club that you tend to sit with every meeting?

"Dave: Just one—Mike O'Brien. Been friends for years.

"You: Do you feel Mike would be a good candidate for . . . ?

"Have three or four specific frames of reference that you know in advance you are going to ask about. All it takes is one name to trigger off an avalanche of referrals."

Bob Burg
www.burg.com

people up and say, "You know, I think we may be able to help each other get more clients. Can we get together and talk about it?" After you have contacted the people you already know, you can add to your circle of referral partners by employing the same strategies you are using to discover and attract clients.

The best referral partnerships are reciprocal. If the two of you are operating in the same market niche, the possibility of referrals flowing both ways is quite high. But even if you can't imagine how you would be able to refer business to the person you are contacting, don't let that stop you. Savvy businesspeople are always looking for qualified professionals to add to their referral bank, because it helps them take good care of their own clients.

When you speak with a potential referral partner, find out as much about the partner's business as you tell her about yours. Exchange marketing literature and several business cards, or familiarize yourself with your partner's website. Ask who would be a good referral for your partner, and explain what type of client you are looking for. End your conversation by asking, "Is there anything else you need to feel confident in referring prospective clients to me?"

Be sure to thank your partners for each and every referral, whether it turns into business for you or not. A prompt thank you will generate more referrals. Keep in touch with your partners over time, just as you do with prospective and former clients. And remember to be on the lookout for referrals you can give to your partners. That's the best way possible to stay in touch with them.

RECIPE: *Networking on the Web*

The Internet has created an abundance of new ways to network without leaving your home or office. For any given market niche, you will find hundreds of websites, blogs, e-zines, and online communities dedicated to serving it. Making a keyword search for sites related to your profession, target market, or area of specialty will point you to many possibilities for interacting with prospects and referral partners online. Here are some of the ways you can use the Web to network:

• *Message Boards and E-Mail Discussion Lists.* Membership organizations, media outlets, vendors, and mailing list services like Yahoo! Groups and Google Groups offer discussion forums on the Web where participation is often free. You can read and post questions and comments on any topic related to the forum's theme. Message boards display questions and answers on the Web, and discussion lists e-mail the

---

Adding More Links to Your Marketing Chain

"If becoming an expert in your field is part of your marketing strategy, online networks give you a much more accessible outlet than the media," suggest Scott Allen and David Teten, authors of *The Virtual Handshake: Opening Doors and Closing Deals Online* (AMACOM, 2005). "You can speak up in a mailing list, discussion forum, or blog, and reach hundreds or thousands of people. Say something useful, original, and profound, and your online comments will get quoted and linked to, reaching even more people.

"Every signature on a post and every online profile is an opportunity to reinforce your brand. Link to your website in your e-mail signature. Link to the communities you belong to from your website. Link to your personal profile page from your community page. Link, link, link. Focus on awareness, not persuasion. Your participation, your signatures, and your profiles will create awareness. Those who are interested will be attracted to you and will come to you for information and assistance.

"A common mistake many marketers make when dealing with online communication is in thinking that it can be turned on and off like an advertising campaign. Online networks are generally not very receptive to marketing messages from brand new members. You must earn the right to talk about your product through participation in and contribution to the community. Long gaps in your participation will be noticed, and if your participation conveniently peaks for the two weeks before your marketing campaign, people will see it as manipulative."

Scott Allen and David Teten
www.thevirtualhandshake.com

---

posts to all the members. Answering a posted question is an excellent way to demonstrate your expertise to a large number of people at once. Don't promote your services directly. Instead, include a brief signature box with your reply that lets members know what you do and how to reach you, for example:

Breeze Carlile, CPCC
It's a Breeze Moving & Organizing · Sausalito, CA
www.itsabreezemoving.com
Home and office relocations and professional organizing

- *Web Chats and Webinars.* These online discussions and presentations on specific themes are typically offered by membership organizations, educational institutions, vendors, and online services such as Talk City or Yahoo! Chat. Unlike online forums, these conversations take place in real time. Some are moderated or have a guest speaker who teaches a class or leads a discussion. Others consist of open conversation among all the participants. In live Web chats, you interact by typing messages on your keyboard that everyone can see on their screen. In a webinar or Web conference, online visuals are combined with an audio presentation or discussion.

In either case, you can often connect privately with other participants during the conversation using an instant messaging option. This allows you to identify people in the public chat room or webinar environment that you would like to meet, then contact them directly to introduce yourself. Again, avoid being overly self-promotional. One appropriate approach is to offer another participant additional resources at no charge in answer to a question he or she asked.

- *Virtual Communities and Social Networking Sites.* Many membership organizations, educational institutions, and vendors offer online communities providing a variety of options for members to connect with each other. Social networking sites such as Ryze or LinkedIn are designed to create a web of personal connections between you and new and existing contacts. These virtual communities allow you to post your profile or a directory listing and have access to the information others post about themselves. You can look up people with whom you might wish to make contact, and in some environments, you can ask a member you already know to introduce you. As with the other forms of online networking, you will get more value from being an active participant, posting on the community's message boards or replying to queries from other members.

- *Blogs.* While publishing your own blog is primarily a writing and publicity tactic, reading and commenting on others' blogs can be a powerful networking approach. When you comment on a blog post, you are making a connection with the author and all of her readers as well. The readers of many blogs become a strong virtual community, following each others' comments as well as the opinions of the blog's author. People reading your thoughts about the blog's topic will become acquainted with your work, and may contact you directly to find out more. Many blog readers are also blog writers. So if your comments are valuable, you may find yourself being quoted or linked to in other blogs.

Before participating in any of these forums, spend some time observing how the existing members tend to communicate. When you have a good sense of the accepted protocol, start making your own contributions. Remember that your goal in online networking is the same as for any other networking environment: building relationships. Serving as a helpful resource and getting to know people better over time will further your marketing goals. Using the community as another advertising medium for your marketing messages will not get you clients, and may even get you banned from membership.

One other online networking approach to consider is asking the owners of other websites that serve your niche to post a link to your site. If you have included helpful resources on your site as discussed earlier in this chapter, others may be happy to point visitors to you for expert help with their problems and goals. More inbound links to your site will increase your "link popularity," one more factor that search engines consider when assigning a relative rank to your site. Some of the people you contact will ask that you place a reciprocal link on your site pointing back to them, which is yet another way to include an element of reciprocity in your networking.

 **Strategy: Public Speaking**

> ### Success Ingredients
>
> Speaking venues
> Speaking topics/bio

RECIPE: *Learning to Speak in Public*

Speaking in public creates positive visibility, boosts your credibility, and establishes you as an expert in your field. It puts you in direct contact with potential clients in such a powerful way that you may find yourself closing a sale before leaving the room. With all the benefits public speaking offers, it's unfortunate that surveys show most people are more afraid of speaking in public than of dying!

If this is true for you, don't include public speaking on your list of strategies just yet. You want to make a good impression on your prospective clients, and you're not going to do that if you're quaking in your boots. Work on getting some practice first. The fact is that the only way to reduce the fear of public speaking is to get experience speaking in public.

Try taking a class at your local community college or a private learning center. Join a local Toastmasters International group, where people meet regularly to practice their speaking and get feedback on their delivery. Or look for a Speaking Circle® in your area. These are groups led by trained facilitators that assist you in developing a natural and authentic speaking style.

You can also work gradually on becoming a better public speaker by gaining more experience. Start by participating in a networking or lead exchange group that requires members to introduce themselves at every meeting. Your next step might be volunteering to host part of a program or make announcements for a group you are part of. After that, you might be ready to serve on a panel, where it is common to speak while staying seated and referring to notes.

Over time, you will get more comfortable at being in front of a group and be able to carry off a solo talk without experiencing panic. You may even grow to like public speaking, and graduate to conducting a breakout session at a conference or even a full-length workshop.

RECIPE: *Finding Places to Speak*

When you are ready to get started with speaking to promote your business, you will first need to locate some **speaking venues**. These are the places, groups, or events where you can give free presentations to prospective clients or referral partners. "Free" doesn't mean there is no admission charge. It means you, the speaker, are not being paid, although in some cases you may receive an honorarium. Here are some suggested venues:

- Chamber of Commerce mixers and workshops
- Service clubs such as Rotary, Lions, and Kiwanis
- Trade and professional association meetings and conferences
- Lectures, workshops, and conferences hosted by educational institutions, community organizations, and affinity groups
- Classes offered by community colleges, resource centers, and private learning centers such as the Learning Annex

- Web chats, webinars, webcasts, podcasts, and teleseminars hosted by membership organizations, educational institutions, and vendors

If some of the entries on this list look suspiciously like those on the list of suggested places to network, you have noticed something very important! Public speaking is superpowered networking. You can speak to the same groups you might otherwise just visit, and you can find them using some of the same resources mentioned for networking and referral building earlier in this chapter. But as the speaker, you will be standing in front of the room instead of sitting in the audience.

As with networking, you don't necessarily have to leave your home or office to be a speaker. In addition to the Web chat and webinar environments described in the earlier section on online networking, webcasts, podcasts, and teleseminars are an increasingly popular format for virtual speaking. Teleseminars, also known as teleclasses or teleforums, are seminars by telephone held on teleconference bridge lines. Dozens or even hundreds of participants listen live and can usually ask questions of the speaker during or after the session. Webcasts and podcasts are one-way presentations delivered over the Internet. Webcasts consist of live or recorded audio and/or video, often combined with other visuals, received on your computer. Podcasts are primarily audio recordings—although video podcasts are increasing—which can be listened to on your computer, but can also be downloaded to a portable MP3 player. Many of these virtual presentations take the form of an interview, where you as the guest expert are asked questions by the regular host.

Keep in mind that the strategy of public speaking has such a high effectiveness rating due to the perceived endorsement of the group hosting the event, and the fact that the host organization invites and enrolls all the participants. Hosting your own speaking program is not a public speaking tactic; it's a promotional event, and is much less effective. So to use the public speaking tactics described in this section, you'll need to find groups to host you as a speaker.

RECIPE: *Getting Booked as a Speaker*

To approach any of these groups about being a speaker, you will need to develop one to three **speaking topics** you would like to present. Your topics should be interesting, distinctive, and showcase your specialized expertise without being excessively self-promotional. They should also allow you to tell stories about your work and include examples of what you have done for clients. In this way, you can deliver valuable content to your audience and promote yourself effectively at the same time.

Most networking groups, service clubs, and professional associations give their guest speakers between 20 and 60 minutes for their talk. Conference breakout sessions and virtual speaking opportunities typically last from 60 to 90 minutes. Workshops and classes can run from 90 minutes to three hours, or even a full day. They can also consist of several sessions offered over a period of days or weeks. You may wish to choose topics for your presentations that can be expanded if you find an opportunity for a longer program, or just stick to topics suitable for a short talk. You will want to give your presentation topics enticing titles that will attract plenty of prospects when printed in a group's newsletter or program announcement.

Write brief descriptions of each topic that will give group organizers enough information to decide if they like it, and can also be used to promote your talk once it is scheduled. (A sample topic description appears in Figure 7-2.)

The second essential tool for getting yourself booked as a speaker is a **speaker's bio** to accompany your topic descriptions. This can be the same professional biography you might display on your website or include in a marketing kit, with one important addition: include any prior speaking experience you have.

If you have only given one or two presentations, you might just add a line to your bio like, "Carlos Maldonado's presentations have been well received by organizations such as the Miami Independent Computer Consultants' Association and the South Florida Technology Consortium." If your speaking experience is more extensive, consider listing the places you have spoken at the bottom of your bio or on a separate page.

It's a good idea to include your website address, if you have one, in the bio you provide. If the group decides to invite you to speak, they will typically print your bio exactly as you wrote it. Then when the group's members see your program advertised, they will know how to find you, and may visit your site even before your talk.

If you have never spoken in public and have no credits to list on your bio, don't let that stop you. If you believe you can do a good job, go for it. You have to give your first talk sometime.

With your topic descriptions and bio prepared, you are ready to start approaching your chosen venues. For networking groups, Chambers of Commerce, service clubs, association meetings, and vendor-sponsored programs, you will typically need to contact the program chairperson or program director. This is sometimes a volunteer working out of his or her own home or office. It's a good idea to find out more about the group before you contact the chairperson. You want to make sure the audience is right for you and be able to tell the chair why your topic would be of interest.

Figure 7-2 Speaking Topic and Bio Example

Speak Like a Pro: Tips and Techniques to Become a Polished Presenter

Wouldn't it be great to be able to stand in front of an audience of hundreds of people and hold them in complete captivation? Would you like to go into a presentation confident that they're going to love you, and overhear comments afterwards such as "He was excellent," or "She made a real connection with her audience"? This program offers proven tips that will help you speak like a pro . . . in a short time!

You will learn how to:

- Develop comfort and confidence
- Write and deliver a winning presentation
- Connect with your audience
- Persuade people to act on what you say
- Enroll clients to purchase your services and products

Your Presenter:

Sandra Schrift has spent 20-plus years working with over 1,500 professional speakers. She founded the first national professional speakers bureau in San Diego in 1982. Today she is a speech coach to executives who want to improve their presentation skills, as well as a career coach to both the emerging and veteran professional speaker who wants to grow a profitable speaking business. Sandra is also the founder of the first virtual university for emerging public speakers, Speakers University, which conducts ongoing teleclasses for anyone, anywhere in the English-speaking world. Find out more about Sandra at www.schrift.com.

Visit the group's website to find out what sort of topics and speakers they usually have. Or, call the group's main number or membership chair and ask for information about the group and their upcoming events. Most groups will mail or e-mail you an information packet or newsletter. This will tell you more about the group and probably also give you the program chair's name, if it isn't on their website. If you still think this group is an appropriate venue for you, contact the program chair directly by phone or e-mail. Don't waste your time sending information to the group's main postal or e-mail address; it will probably be discarded.

If the program chair expresses interest, find out how far ahead the group is scheduling speakers, and send the chairperson your topics and bio. Then follow up after an appropriate interval to see if you are able to get yourself on the program.

With conferences, educational institutions, resource centers, and private learning centers, study last year's schedule or the current catalog before you contact them. If they already have a program on your topic, see if you can find a new and different angle that hasn't yet been covered. When you're sure you have something fresh to propose, call the department chair or program director to see if the organization is interested. You will probably be asked to submit a proposal, for which the group may or may not have written guidelines. If no guidelines are available, send a description of your proposed topic and speaker's bio, with a cover letter explaining why you think this topic will be popular with the organization's audience. And don't forget to follow up.

 Strategy: Writing and Publicity

> ### *Success Ingredients*
>
> Writing venues
>
> Article or query letter
>
> Publicity venues
>
> Press release/media kit
>
> Blog concept/topics

RECIPE: *Writing Articles or Tips*

Just like public speaking, writing **articles or tips** for your market niche can help you become more credible as well as more visible. A well-written article or a series of useful tips on a subject of interest to your market will get their attention, demonstrate your expertise, and increase your name recognition. You can publish articles or tips in a wide variety of ways:

- Submit your articles to magazines, trade journals, newspapers, websites, newsletters, and e-zines.

Tip-Top Talk Topics

"The most common response I hear when a successful businessperson is asked to speak is, 'What would I talk about?'" reports Roseann Sullivan, a public speaking trainer and coach. Roseann suggests, "Talk about the things people ask you about at parties. What aspect of your work do you find yourself spending hours of your free time discussing? What information do you have that can solve people's problems? A tax attorney could talk about winning an audit and a publicist about getting free publicity.

"Think beyond the predictable. Too many unknowing professionals waste time and money developing overdone presentations. For example, if you are a realtor, avoid the temptation to give a predictable presentation on buying your first home. Do something different, like 'how to escape the big city.' Unconventional topics will draw crowds of prospects to your program.

"When deciding on your topic and approach, focus on giving valuable information and exceeding the expectations of your audience. Impart some wisdom to them, so that even if they don't become your clients, your presentation makes an impact. Create goodwill by always giving 110 percent. You already know the importance of word-of-mouth marketing, so make sure there are lots of good words floating around about you."

Roseann Sullivan

- Publish articles or tips in your own e-zine or blog, and on your website.

- Write a regular column for a publication or website.

- Include copies of your articles in your marketing kit or media kit.

- Send copies of (or links to) an article to people on your follow-up list with a "thought-you-would-be-interested" note.

- Send copies to your clients with your next invoice.

- Use articles or a collection of tips as a handout at trade shows and speaking engagements.

- When you speak to a group, offer to send articles or tips to any-one who gives you a business card.

- Leave an article behind with prospects after you make a presen-tation or include one with a proposal.

- Frame your published article and hang it on your office wall.

- Compile your articles or tips into a free booklet or e-book that you give to prospects.

The first step in getting an article published beyond your own newsletter or website is to identify appropriate **writing venues**. What print publications and e-zines do the people in your market niche read? What websites do they visit? Ask your clients and prospects what publi-cations they subscribe to or regularly buy. Notice which periodicals are lying on their desks or poking out of their briefcases, and which e-zines they forward to you. For print publications, you can look up possible ven-ues in directories for writers, such as those published by Writer's Market. For e-zines and websites, you can look them up online by doing keyword searches for your target market or professional specialty.

As with public speaking, the best topics for your articles will be those that allow you to share valuable information with your audience, but are not self-promotional in nature. An article that is little more than a sales pitch for your services won't find a publisher.

If you are new to getting your writing published, start with publica-tions and websites that don't require much writing experience. Associa-tion newsletters are an excellent first target, as are the newsletters and e-zines of colleagues, referral partners, and vendors in your niche. Web-sites that collect articles for the free use of online editors and publishers (e.g., Article City or Ezine Articles™) will accept articles from first-time authors. Other possibilities are employee newsletters, community news-papers, or advertising periodicals, like those that list homes for sale or job openings. Once you have been published in a few venues like these, you will have a track record as a writer and be able to approach print publications with a larger circulation and websites with a higher profile.

In most cases, you won't be paid for your articles. What you will re-ceive, however, is an extended byline or "bio slug" printed at the end of your article, where you can describe your professional services and give your phone number and/or website address.

Some venues will be happy to accept a completed article or allow you to pitch your article idea with a phone call or brief e-mail. Other publications, particularly the more prestigious ones, will require a **query letter**. If you're not sure what a particular venue requires, look for editorial guidelines on its website, or contact the appropriate editor and ask. Most print publications list the name and department of each editor in a box near the table of contents, inside the front cover, or for newspapers, in the editorial section.

If you contact the editor by phone, be prepared to pitch your article idea on the spot. Describe your proposed topic, explain why it is of interest to readers, and tell why you should be the one who writes it. A brief e-mail query should contain the same details. If you're convincing enough, some publications will give you the assignment right then. Others will ask you to send a formal query letter and include some samples of your writing.

If a publication's guidelines request that you query, don't try to skip this step by sending a completed article in the hope that the publication will print it. It's likely the editor won't even look at it, and you will have wasted your time.

A query letter should begin with a strong lead paragraph, written just as if it were the opening paragraph of the actual article. You want it to capture the editor's interest, introduce your topic, and show that you can write. Continue the letter by describing two or three key points you intend to have your article make. Then propose the article itself: "I would like to write a 1,500-word article on the benefits to employers of integrated disability management programs. I plan to interview three employers who have experienced significant cost reductions . . ."

Conclude the letter with a brief description of your background that indicates why you are qualified to write the article. If you have previously been published, send along two sample articles, or links to them, with your letter. E-mail submissions are most common these days, but if you are querying by mail, send a self-addressed, stamped envelope for the editor to reply.

The elapsed time it takes editors to respond to a query varies widely. Follow up after 30 days if you haven't heard anything. If the publication you are querying requests "first rights" for the articles it publishes, don't send the same query to another editor until you are sure the first one doesn't want it.

Once you have had an article published in one venue, don't stop there. Many publications and websites are happy to accept previously published articles. When you have an article published, make sure you are agreeing to give the publication only first rights or one-time rights. Then you can get a great deal of mileage out of the same piece by submitting it over and over to different venues. Again, check the editorial

---

Virtual Customers Have Real Expectations

"This is the age of the virtual customer," declares Steven Van Yoder, author of *Get Slightly Famous* (Bay Tree, 2003). "Although the Internet has made it perfectly reasonable to land a major client you've never met in person, it has also created new expectations.

"Prospects now 'Google' around to find someone with your skills. They expect you to make a good virtual case for yourself. If you appear lackluster compared to your competitors, you will lose the potential client. Think about it. You have probably used the Internet to research a company or person you're considering doing business with. Certainly potential clients are checking you out on-line, too.

"Publishing articles online draws upon and displays your expertise by providing useful information that website visitors are actively seeking out. Online articles position you as an expert in your field and convey a level of authority that establishes trust and sets the stage for sales.

"When high-traffic, high-credibility websites and e-zines publish your articles, you ride on the coattails of their loyal relationships with readers. Your articles are seen by visitors as referrals from trusted friends.

"Some of the most prime real estate in the world these days is at the top of the search engine listings. The most widely used search engines rank websites by the quantity of other websites that link to them. This means that every article you publish that links to your website can improve your search engine rankings.

"The only way to be truly successful in business is by establishing a good reputation. And understanding the way business has shifted in the Internet age can help you bring the potential of marketing your business into the virtual world."

Steven Van Yoder
www.getslightlyfamous.com

---

guidelines. If first rights are not required, you can offer articles that have been previously published.

After you have successfully placed a number of articles, you might consider finding a venue for an ongoing column. Landing a regular column with a publication or website respected by your target market is a major milestone in establishing your expertise, and can significantly boost your name recognition.

RECIPE: *Getting Media Publicity*

Attracting the attention of the print, broadcast, and Web media can get you quoted, interviewed, or profiled. When prospective clients see you featured in the news, your credibility and name recognition may greatly increase. The more visible you are in your profession, the more likely it is that the media will contact you, but don't just sit back and wait. Generating publicity can be relatively easy, particularly if you start with smaller outlets.

Begin by identifying the best **publicity venues**—places your market niche and referral partners will be likely to notice an article or interview about you. Here are some suggestions, beginning with some of the easier targets for your first publicity attempt:

- Newsletter or e-zine of a professional association or networking group of which you are a member
- Alumni newsletter for your school or college
- Newsletter of an organization you volunteer for
- Local newspaper for your neighborhood or town
- Local trade journal for your profession
- Local radio or cable television show that focuses on a topic in your area of expertise
- Local or regional magazine that covers topics you can speak about
- Website that covers news, events, and personalities for your market niche
- Freelance journalists who write about your field
- Daily newspaper for your metropolitan area
- Local television news, magazine, or talk show
- National trade journal for your profession
- Nationally syndicated radio show
- National magazine that covers topics you can speak about
- Web media that cover news, events, and personalities nationally or internationally

- National print news media (e.g., *Newsweek*, *Wall Street Journal*)
- National wire service (e.g., Associated Press, Reuters)
- National television news, magazine, or talk show

For newsletters, magazines, newspapers, and most Web media, you will need the name of the appropriate editor. For radio, television, and Web broadcasts, you will need the appropriate producer's name. With news media, you can also approach reporters who cover the topic you are seeking publicity about. You can usually get these names by reading, watching, or listening to the publication or program you plan to approach (which is a good idea anyway). You can also look them up in directories like *Bacon's Publicity Checker* or search the media outlet's web site.

An essential tool for approaching the media is a well-written **press release** or pitch letter, which may be one component of a complete **media kit**. A press release is a one- or two-page bulletin that you send to the media to announce news or alert them to a story. Successful releases issued by service professionals generally fall into one of three categories:

1. *News.* You are announcing something the venues you are approaching will consider newsworthy. For an association newsletter or neighborhood newspaper, this might be the opening of your business or landing a new client. For larger media, you need bigger news, such as publication of a book or survey, an invention or discovery, or winning an award. If you don't have a major event like this to announce, don't despair. Consider what kind of problems your market niche is currently experiencing that you have a solution for. Is there a potential news story in your solution?

2. *Commentary.* This type of release is positioning you as an expert on a currently hot topic. Or, instead of a release, you might choose to write a pitch letter where you propose yourself as an interview subject or suggest a feature story about your business. "Sandwich Generation Feeling the Squeeze" could be the headline for a geriatric care consultant's release or the opening hook in her pitch letter. Then describe the situation that makes your comments topical, give a brief summary of your expertise, and add a pithy quote from you on the topic.

3. *Tips article.* Many publications will print your press release verbatim if it is written in the form of a brief article of significant interest to their readers. Articles with a seasonal angle can be very successful. A

personal shopper might write 300 words on "How to Buy Lingerie for Your Valentine," with herself as the expert quoted in the article.

Figure 7-3 illustrates a sample press release of the news variety to show you the format and style the media expects.

Figure 7-3 Press Release Example

FOR IMMEDIATE RELEASE

Contact: Barbara McDonald
Phone: (510) 282-9817
E-mail: logolady1@aol.com

SELF-TAUGHT DESIGNER WINS BAY AREA LOGO DESIGN CONTEST

A logo created by Oakland-based graphic designer Barbara McDonald was chosen over more than 250 entries received in a design contest sponsored by The San Francisco Foundation. The contest, open to Bay Area artists of all types, challenged entrants to design a new logo for The San Francisco Foundation, an organization beginning its fiftieth year of service to Bay Area communities.

The San Francisco Foundation, which awards grants to nonprofit organizations in economic development, education, environment, culture, immigration, and youth, awarded McDonald $6,000 for her winning entry and will use it on all of its printed materials, signage, and website. "I was thrilled to have just made it to the finals of the contest," said McDonald, "but then to have my logo chosen by a prestigious organization like The San Francisco Foundation was quite an honor for me."

A self-taught artist, McDonald started her career painting sets and props for the Disney Design Center, then moved into graphic design while working for a large sign company in Los Angeles. Her business, Native Design, was founded in 1994, and her clients range from small business owners like herself to local restaurants like Picante and Jupiter, and medium-sized companies like The California Academy of Family Physicians.

"It has always been important for me to work with people and organizations who make a positive contribution to the community, and The San Francisco Foundation is the epitome of that type of client," stated McDonald.

Making the News

"In public relations, your job is to define your expertise to the media," advises Jill Lublin, co-author of *Guerrilla Publicity* (Adams Media, 2002) and *Networking Magic* (Adams Media, 2004). "One of my clients is an industrial designer for corporations—interesting, but not exciting. It turns out he runs his successful company as a 'virtual corporation,' so he became an expert on that topic. That caught the media's attention, and he has been featured nationally in newspapers, radio, and television.

"Here are some key points to remember in using public relations:

1. Be ready to define your business concisely. Prepare a 30-second introduction that includes your business, your name, and a benefit of doing business with you.

2. Know who your public is, and target your audience. Yes, the universe can be your audience, but it's very expensive to market to. Define your audience with demographics.

3. Tell your story. Why would someone want to do business with you? Find out what makes you the most interesting and relates to the largest number of people.

4. Write a press release that answers the who, what, where, when, and why of your story. A well-written, concise release with an exciting lead paragraph will increase your chances.

5. Send your release to a researched media list. Have as many names as possible that are relevant to your topic including business editors, features editors, columnists, and producers.

6. Follow up your release with phone calls. Have alternative pitches ready in case your media contact doesn't like the first one. Be precise and to the point when leaving a message.

"The media is accessible. We, the public, create stories. What you see in the news is about people like you and me. Read the paper you will be talking to, watch the television show, or listen to the radio program to see where you can fit in to make some news of your own."

Jill Lublin
www.jilllublin.com

When you are angling for a feature article about you or a live interview on radio, TV, or the Web, you will want to supplement your press release with other material, turning it into a complete **media kit**. This should be sent to media contacts only after they have expressed some interest, or it will probably end up in the wastebasket. Here are some ideas for what your kit might include:

- One-page biography of yourself
- Profile of your company or fact sheet about your work
- Photograph of you (action photos are best)
- Samples of other press you have received
- Articles you have published
- Testimonials from clients or endorsements from influential people
- Sample questions and answers for an interview
- Audio or video recording of a previous interview

Any of this material can also be made available on your website in a "press room" section, and you can provide links to it instead of sending the material itself.

Most media outlets now accept press releases and pitch letters by e-mail, although a few still prefer postal mail. Sending releases by fax should be your last choice, as these are often ignored. Just as you should do when approaching prospective clients, call your media contacts after sending them a release. Pitch your story on the phone and try to get them interested. If they want your media kit, ask how they would like to receive it.

Learning how to write an effective release, compiling a media list, sending out all those releases, and pitching your story to the media may be more work than you want to tackle by yourself. Hiring a full-service publicist can be expensive, but you might decide to use the services of a public relations consultant a la carte, just to write your release, for example. There are also services that will distribute your press release to their media subscribers for a fee.

One final approach to gaining visibility in the media is to write to editors and producers who serve your market niche. Commenting on a published piece or broadcast story can sometimes get your letter printed or read on the air. But it can also get you into the editor's or producer's contact database. Conclude your letter or e-mail with your contact information and an invitation like this: "The next time you run a story on carpal tunnel syndrome or repetitive strain injuries, please feel free to contact me for background information. I am an ergonomics consultant who specializes in helping heavy keyboard users set up their offices to avoid strain and injury."

RECIPE: *Publish Your Own Writing with a Blog*

Publishing a blog allows you to combine both writing and publicity techniques in one activity. As a blog author, you are publishing your own stories on the Web. So you are not only the writer, you are also the media outlet.

Blogs, an abbreviation that has evolved from "weblogs," are websites where you post articles, tips, comments, essays, and resource links in a journal format. Some blogs also include photos, graphic images, and audio or video clips. Blogs can help you fill the pipeline by attracting new clients who find you through search engines or links from other sites and blogs. They are also an excellent follow-up tool, and you'll read more about that in Chapter 8.

To start authoring your own blog, you will need a **blog concept** and a series of **blog topics**. The concept for your blog should be a sustainable theme of continuing interest to your market niche. Coin a clever or evocative title for your blog that expresses the theme. For example, a communication skills trainer could name her blog "Can We Talk?" and a hypnotherapist could name his "Getting Out of the Habit."

Visit several blogs aimed at your market niche to see what topics others are writing about. You'll discover that some blog posts are lengthy articles or essays, and others are brief comments or tips. Many blog posts contain links pointing readers to articles, books, news, resource sites, and items written by other bloggers. You'll also notice that authoring a blog takes commitment. Keeping your blog up to date will require posting to it regularly, probably once per week at minimum. You will need to develop a substantial number of topics to begin with, and keep coming up with new ones over time.

You can create and update your blog using blogging software (e.g., Blogger or Typepad). Some software is free to use and other systems charge a fee. Many blogging systems are Web-based applications, so there is no software to install. A blog can be hosted on your own existing website or you can set up a special site just for your blog. Many blogging systems offer free hosting if you are willing to display ads on your blog.

Like any other website, a blog must be promoted in order to receive a lot of traffic. But the good news about blogs is that they are naturally rich in keywords relevant to your market niche, so they often achieve good placement in search engines without additional effort on your part. Also, as you make new posts, your older posts will be archived, automatically creating multiple pages that the search engines will index. If the topics you write on are interesting, informative, and useful to people in your niche, other sites and bloggers will link to your blog, sending more traffic your way.

When you first launch your blog, be sure to announce it to your clients, prospects, colleagues, and referral partners. Mention it in all your marketing materials, and link to it from your e-mail signature and any other websites you maintain.

If setting up a blog for the first time seems too technically complex, hire someone to help you with installation. After your blog has been created, you should have no trouble posting to it without assistance.

 **Strategy: Promotional Events**

Success Ingredients

Promotion concept

Promotion plan

RECIPE: *Putting on a Show*

Organizing or participating in a promotional event can consume a significant amount of time and money. Before making a commitment to put on a show, check your budget. Add up all the costs of producing the event, promoting it, and making a good showing at it. Divide the total by the number of clients you can honestly expect to get as a result of the event, to see how much each client is going to cost you. Do you still think it's worth it? Can you think of an easier or cheaper way to get the same number of clients?

Only if your event passes this test should you go ahead with it. Many professionals have found exhibit booths at trade shows to be an expensive mistake. On the other hand, free demonstrations or low-cost workshops have been a solid source of clients for others. Ask your colleagues what has worked, and not worked, for them.

To create or be part of a promotional event, a **promotion concept** is the starting place. Here are some ideas for promotional events you might consider:

- Display table at your networking group's business fair or expo
- Exhibit booth or demonstration at a trade show, vendor fair, or community event aimed at your market niche
- Hosting a networking event, reception, or open house at your place of business
- Being a sponsor for a fundraising event or award ceremony
- Demonstrating or exhibiting your work in your office or studio by invitation
- Offering a free or low-cost workshop to your target audience
- Sponsoring a teleclass, teleseminar series, or webinar for clients and prospects

When you have come up with a concept that you like and tested its financial viability, you're ready to make a **promotion plan**. The more elaborate your event is, the more extensive your planning needs. Here are some elements your plan might include:

- *Advance Publicity*. Even if the event is sponsored by someone else, you will get more mileage from it if you invite your own prospects to attend. Many trade shows and fundraisers will provide you with postcards, flyers, an e-mail announcement, or a website banner you can use to spread the word. If you are the sponsor, evaluate all the marketing techniques at your disposal to determine what combination might work the best. You may want to mail or e-mail invitations, post flyers, issue press releases, ask colleagues to send announcements to their mailing lists, or purchase ad space.

- *Exhibit Booth*. Your booth or display table should reflect your level of professionalism and visually display your expertise. A banner or sign board will make your exhibit more visible. Use photographs, testimonial letters, press clippings, and samples of your work to make what you do as tangible as possible. Try to find out what sort of displays any other exhibitors will have. You don't want to look cheap or unprepared by comparison.

- *Marketing Literature*. If you exhibit at a large event, be prepared to give away many copies of your literature. Some attendees make a habit of taking something from each booth, regardless of whether they are actually interested. It's a good idea to have a relatively inexpensive piece available for the taking, and keep your more costly brochure or marketing kit behind the table to give to serious prospects.

• *Script, Outline, or Presentation System.* If you are offering a workshop or teleclass, design a program that will give your audience valuable information whether or not they decide to do business with you. Practice using any needed technology, such as a teleconference bridge or Power-Point presentation. For an exhibit, prepare in advance what you will say to people who come by your booth. Think of one good qualifying question you can ask at the outset of a conversation to see if the person you are speaking with is a prospect. Create a fact sheet for any helpers you will have so they can answer predictable questions. If you will be conducting a demonstration, script and rehearse it. You will be the star of this show, and you don't want to flop.

• *Capturing Leads.* The traditional way to capture the contact information of people who attend an event is to collect business cards for a drawing or names for your mailing list. Offering a free gift can result in collecting a large number of names with no way of knowing who is a legitimate prospect. Insert a qualifier into your drawing: Ask people to answer a qualifying question on the back of their card before dropping it in. To save time at an exhibit booth, use two stickers of different colors to indicate yes or no.

• *Logistical Details.* Plan ahead for all the small things that can make your event more successful—for example, extra helpers, extension cords, refreshments, giveaways, pens and paper, small bills to make change, and name tags. Try to have backup arrangements in case anything goes wrong, like an extra battery for your laptop or your presentation saved to a CD. If all the details are handled, you can concentrate on making a good impression.

 Strategy: Advertising

> ### *Success Ingredients*
>
> Advertising venues
> Flyer venues
> Ad copy, layout, or script

RECIPE: *Making Advertising Work*

There are a number of reasons why advertising is last on the list of marketing strategies for professional services. First, there's the know, like, and trust factor. Advertising is not an effective way to gain a prospective client's trust. Second, advertising generates leads, not sales. People calling you or visiting your website because they saw an ad will take much more convincing than prospects who are referred to you. They will be more likely to bargain for a lower price, ask for references, or require a written proposal and lengthy sales cycle than will people who know you better.

Third, like any other marketing strategy, advertising must be done repeatedly to have an effect. Ongoing advertising can be very expensive. H & R Block can afford to advertise their tax preparation services because they have an enormous staff in many locations waiting to serve clients. The cost of this advertising is reasonable when divided by that many people, all working to generate revenue. But a two-person accounting office just can't generate enough revenue to pay for an extensive advertising campaign.

The reality is that the other five strategies all attract more prospects who become clients—and at a lower price—than advertising does for the vast majority of professionals. Sure, advertising might bring you some clients, but your objective is to get the best result with the least investment of time and money.

And advertising is an investment—a high-risk investment. In using it, you should follow the same steps as you would to invest in anything:

1. Analyze your options carefully.

2. Choose the vehicle with the highest return at the lowest cost.

3. Don't invest what you can't afford to lose.

To examine the potential return on your advertising investment, ask yourself these questions:

- How many leads do you expect your ads to generate?
- What will each lead cost you?
- How many will become clients?
- What will be the dollar value of those closed sales?
- Is there a cheaper way you could generate the same amount of revenue?

• How much can you really afford to spend?

Once you have made the commitment to advertise, and know how much you can afford to invest, here are some suggestions for getting the most from your advertising dollar:

• *Target the right audience.* The narrower your target, the better. Specialized publications and websites are often cheaper to advertise with than the ones with wide appeal. Targeting also permits you to tailor your ad for the people most likely to buy.

• *Place your ad where they "shop."* When is it most likely that a client will realize she needs you? Where might she be looking at that time? If you are a résumé writer, you can advertise in your neighborhood newspaper and hope that people about to start a job search run across your ad. But it's more likely that local job seekers would find you in the Yellow Pages.

• *Request an immediate response.* Institutional advertising is for the big guys. You really can't afford to advertise just for name recognition; you need a direct response. A financial planner might headline an online ad: "How much savings will you need to retire? Click here to find out with our free online calculator."

• *Repeat; don't scatter.* People often don't respond the first, second, or tenth time they see your ad, so give them more chances. When your budget is limited, buy repeat ads in the same venue, not one ad in several different ones. Make sure people see your ad often. For the same money that a large display ad in the newspaper would cost once per quarter, you could probably run a classified ad every week.

• *Track and adjust.* Keep track of the response to every ad—not just the volume of calls or site visitors, but the value of the sales they generate. To do this, you will need to keep accurate records of where every prospect comes from, and how much each one spends with you. If an ad isn't bringing you paying clients after you have run it several times, dump it, even if you're getting plenty of inquiries. Revisit the points above, and see if you can come closer to your target, where they shop, and what will prompt a response. And if an ad is working for you, don't change it. You will get tired of your ads long before your clients do.

RECIPE: *Distributing Flyers*

Flyers are one of the most inexpensive forms of advertising, and an appropriate medium for many professionals marketing to consumers and small businesses. If you are already doing a fair amount of networking and referral building, you may often find yourself in places where you can hand out, post, or display flyers to increase your visibility and generate new inquiries. Likely **flyer venues** include the following places:

- *Networking Events.* You may be able to hand out flyers when you introduce yourself, leave them on a table for people to pick up, or place one on each chair. If you don't know what the group's rules are, be sure to ask first so you don't offend anyone.

- *Trade Shows.* If you have a booth, your flyers will be there, of course. If you don't, you could ask a referral partner to display flyers for you. Many shows prohibit the distribution of flyers by nonexhibitors, but creative marketers have been known to pass out flyers outside the show.

- *Educational Institutions, Association Headquarters, Health Practitioners' Offices, Resource Centers, and Community Gathering Places.* Many have bulletin boards, resource binders, waiting room counters, or literature racks where your flyers could be seen or picked up.

The **ad copy** and **layout** of your flyer will be important to its effectiveness. Special offers such as "15% discount for appointments scheduled before Oct. 31" or "free consultation with this flyer" can encourage people to call. Flyers that advertise only one service at a time get more response than those that contain a laundry list of everything you have available.

The most common flyer design is to use a full page and print on one side of colored paper stock. But you could also print your flyer on two sides and fold it into thirds to create the look of a brochure. Or, you could print on card stock and cut your page in half or thirds to create smaller-sized coupons or fact sheets.

The design and printing of your flyer should reflect your level of professionalism. If your flyer looks homemade, that's how people will view your service. Consider investing a few extra dollars in having your flyer professionally designed. For small quantities, printing flyers on your laser or inkjet printer may be an acceptable solution. For larger numbers, you will want to have your flyers photocopied or printed. Either way, be sure the paper stock and colors you use project the image that you want.

RECIPE: *Sending Direct Mail*

The difference between direct mail and sending personal letters to prospective clients is the level of individual attention you give each prospect and the volume of marketing pieces you send. The difference in the impact these two tactics have can be significant. Think of yourself as an example. How much of the mail arriving at your door do you actually read? Do those marketing letters you get with your name inserted fool you into thinking the letter was written just for you? Who are you more likely to contact—someone who sent you a coupon in the mail or someone who was recommended by a friend?

Many people who receive a lot of mail routinely throw away envelopes from senders they don't recognize. If they do hang on to your mailing, it will probably be sitting at the bottom of a stack somewhere. This is why calling before you send a personal letter is so important. It may be the only way to save your letter from the circular file. And calling after you send it is the only way to know if it was read.

Sending a generic marketing piece to a large mailing list is much better used as a follow-up technique than for filling the pipeline. (See Chapter 8 for more about this.) If despite these warnings you want to try using direct mail as your first approach to a cold list, consider working with a marketing communications specialist to design the **ad copy** and **layout** for your mailing. Getting professional help to compose your letter, design your mailer, or lay out your postcard can greatly increase its effectiveness.

Try offering a free gift, discount coupon, complimentary consultation, or other time-limited offer as an incentive for the recipient to call you or visit your website. If you are sending a letter, paying someone to hand-address the envelopes is one way to increase the odds of your letters being opened. Printing a teaser on the outside—"Look inside for your free gift"—is another. Just be sure whatever tricks you use to get your mailing piece noticed reflect the professional image you want to present.

RECIPE: *Directory Advertising*

One of the most popular **advertising venues** for service businesses is the advertising directory. This category includes the Yellow Pages produced by your local phone company; similar directories produced by competing groups; membership directories and resource guides printed by associations and unions; and affinity group directories, such as the Hispanic Yellow Pages.

There are really only two reasons to advertise in a particular directory:

1. You expect that potential clients will be looking for your service in that directory at the time they are ready to buy.

2. It is a standard practice in your industry to be listed in that directory, so it would detract from your credibility if you weren't included.

When advertising solely for the second reason, there's no point in buying a big ad. Just pay for the basic listing. Don't worry about impressing potential buyers with the size of your ad. Even well-established companies often keep this type of ad quite small.

When you are advertising for reason 1, it's important that your **ad copy** and **layout** be designed to catch the eye of your best prospects. Study the existing ads in your category carefully. Make yours stand out by using unique graphics or an intriguing headline. If there are many large ads in your category already, recognize that a smaller ad will have a hard time competing.

Rather than packing lots of information into your ad, focus on one key benefit you provide or one problem you solve for your clients. On a page filled with ads for psychotherapy, most of which mention depression, relationship problems, and eating disorders, an ad highlighting "recovery from trauma" will stand out and attract someone for whom this is an issue. If you can't decide which of your services to promote, pick the one no one else is advertising. Remember that the sole purpose of an ad like this is to make your phone ring.

Beware of new, untested directories. Just because a distributor prints 50,000 copies doesn't mean anyone will be reading them.

RECIPE: *Print Advertising*

The variety of **advertising venues** available in print is truly enormous. You can place display, classified, or calendar listing ads in newspapers, magazines, newsletters, trade journals, or event programs. How do you choose? This is where targeting is extremely important. There's no point in placing an ad in a publication your target market doesn't read. You also may find that periodicals with a large circulation are far too expensive for you to consider, while specialized publications aimed only at your market are more affordable.

Look for venues where you could be the only advertiser in your category, or offer something completely unique. A career counselor might get a good response from a small classified above the "Help Wanted" section that read, "Looking for something different? I can help you find meaningful work. Call for a free newsletter."

Use the services of a graphic designer, copywriter, or marketing communications professional to make sure your **ad copy** and **layout** will attract attention. Just as in directory advertising, narrow the focus of your ad to one key point that will resonate with your best prospective clients.

The headline of your ad is the most important part of its design. If the headline doesn't attract attention, your ad won't be read. Inexperienced advertisers often make the mistake of headlining their ad with the name of their company. But no one cares who your company is unless they need what you have to offer.

Effective headlines directly address a prospect's needs by stating a principal benefit of the service being offered, or mentioning a problem the prospect may have. Here are some examples:

Does Your Computer Give You a Pain in the Neck?

Affordable Bankruptcy

How Safe Are Your Investments?

Adults with Attention Deficit Disorder

Health Insurance at a Price that Won't Make You Sick

Relationship Troubles?

Remember to track the results of every ad you run carefully. It's the only way you will know what's working for you and what isn't.

RECIPE: *Advertising on the Web*

There are probably as many different ways to advertise on the Internet as there are in all of the other available media combined. You can send bulk e-mail to thousands of recipients, pay for placement in Web directories, buy an ad on a Web broadcast, purchase banner ads on websites and in e-zines, or use pay-per-click ads to focus the reach of your advertising and pay only for the response you get.

Before you start advertising on the Web, make sure your website does a good job of selling your services. There's no point in paying to get more traffic if prospects don't buy from you after they visit. You may want to read more about how your site can do better at converting visitors to buyers in Chapters 9 and 10.

Here are some suggestions for getting the most out of Web advertising:

• *Bulk E-Mail.* Sending unsolicited generic e-mails to large groups of people who don't know you is a waste of your time and money, and in some cases may be a violation of the law. It can also backfire dra-

Ads Should Win Rewards, Not Awards

Bob Bly is the author of more than 50 books including *The Copywriter's Handbook* (Owl, 1990) and *The Online Copywriter's Handbook* (McGraw-Hill, 2003). Bob advises: "To define what constitutes good print advertising, we begin with what a good print ad is not: It is not creative for the sake of being creative. It is not designed to please copywriters, art directors, agency presidents, or even clients. Its main purpose is not to entertain, win awards, or shout at the readers, 'I am an *ad*. Don't you admire my fine writing, bold graphics, and clever concept?' In other words, ignore most of what you would learn as a student in any basic advertising class or as a trainee in one of the big Madison Avenue consumer ad agencies.

"As for what an ad *should* be, here are some characteristics shared by successful direct response print ads:

1. They stress a benefit. The main selling proposition is not cleverly hidden but is made immediately clear.

2. They arouse curiosity and invite readership. The key here is not to be outrageous but to address the strongest interests and concerns of your target audience.

3. They provide information. Ads that provide information the reader wants get higher readership and better response.

4. They have a strong free offer. Good ads tell the reader the next step in the buying process and encourage him to take it *now*.

"All ads should have an offer, because the offer generates immediate response from prospects who are ready to buy now or at least thinking about buying. Without an offer, these 'urgent' prospects are not encouraged to reach out to you, and you lose many potential clients."

Robert W. Bly
www.bly.com

matically when prospects are annoyed by receiving your messages. It is possible to purchase "opt-in" lists of people who have supposedly agreed to receive bulk e-mail on certain subjects, but not all of these lists are legitimate. A much wiser use of e-mail is to make a personal approach to individual prospects as described at the beginning of this

The More Things Change, the More They Stay the Same

1. The first time a man looks at an advertisement, he does not see it.
2. The second time, he does not notice it.
3. The third time, he is conscious of its existence.
4. The fourth time, he faintly remembers having seen it before.
5. The fifth time, he reads it.
6. The sixth time, he turns up his nose at it.
7. The seventh time, he reads it through and says, "Oh brother!"
8. The eighth time, he says, "Here's that confounded thing again!"
9. The ninth time, he wonders if it amounts to anything.
10. The tenth time, he asks his neighbor if he has tried it.
11. The eleventh time, he wonders how the advertiser makes it pay.
12. The twelfth time, he thinks it must be a good thing.
13. The thirteenth time, he thinks perhaps it might be worth something.
14. The fourteenth time, he remembers wanting such a thing a long time.
15. The fifteenth time, he is tantalized because he cannot afford to buy it.
16. The sixteenth time, he thinks he will buy it some day.
17. The seventeenth time, he makes a memorandum to buy it.
18. The eighteenth time, he swears at his poverty.
19. The nineteenth time, he counts his money carefully.
20. The twentieth time he sees the ad, he buys what it is offering.

Written in 1885 by Thomas Smith, London, England.

chapter, or to use it as a follow-up technique with your own in-house mailing list.

- *Web Directories.* The major Web directories are often referred to as search engines, but they are not the same. Directories are compiled into categories by humans, while search engine listings are created by automated systems. Some directories offer free listings (e.g., Open Directory) but most charge a fee for businesses to be listed (e.g., LookSmart). As of this writing, Yahoo! offers both options: they will index your site at no charge in their search engine listings, but will charge to include your site in their business directory. There are also many niche-specific Web directories or online malls. For example, a wedding planner could advertise in WeddingChannel, or an acupuncturist could purchase a listing in Acufinder.

To decide if advertising in a Web directory makes sense for you, review the suggestions under "Directory Advertising" earlier in this chapter. You might also consider asking some colleagues what their experience has been with advertising in similar directories.

- *Web Broadcasts.* The Web offers both live and recorded audio and video programming, often called Internet radio or Internet TV. Many of these are regularly broadcast radio and TV programs being made available on the Web, but others are produced just for Internet listeners and viewers. To consider whether you should be an Internet radio or TV advertiser, read the section on "Radio and TV Advertising" that follows.

- *Banner Ads.* These colorful ads on websites and in e-zines encourage visitors to click on them to visit your website. Just like print ads, the most effective ones make a special offer to encourage response. Some advertising venues will charge you a flat fee to run your ad for a certain period of time, others will charge based on the number of "impressions" your ad receives (i.e., the number of people who view it), and still others will charge for "click-throughs" (i.e., the number of people who click on it).

To evaluate using banner ads for which you pay a flat fee or per-impression fee, review the tips under "Print Advertising" earlier in this chapter. For ads charging per click, see below.

- *Pay-Per-Click Ads.* These are text or graphic ads for which you pay a fee every time someone clicks on the ad to visit your website. Sometimes these ads appear in a fixed location, such as a certain page on a website or in an e-zine. Other pay-per-click ads are context-sensitive (e.g., Google AdWords). This means they are displayed on search engine pages and/or a wide variety of advertising-supported sites where keywords related to your service are in use. For example, a project management consultant could purchase a pay-per-click ad for the keyword phrase "project management" and agree to pay a maximum of $2.00 every time a visitor clicked through to visit her site. When someone searched for "project management" using the search engine from whom the consultant purchased the ad, the consultant's ad would appear on the results page as a sponsored listing. The consultant could also opt to have her ad appear on advertising-supported websites with related content. These could include blogs about project management, project management resource sites, and more.

The key to determining whether pay-per-click advertising is a good choice for you is to know the true value of a click. If 1,000 people click on the project management consultant's ad, it will cost her $2,000. If only one of those people hires her for a $20,000 project, her ad will have been worth the investment. But if all of those visitors turn out to be surfing the Web looking for free resources on project management, her ad will have been an expensive mistake. Many pay-per-click advertising vendors offer a user guide to help you decide how much you can realistically afford to pay. Be sure to weigh all the factors carefully before agreeing to a contract.

RECIPE: *Radio and TV Advertising*

Can you afford to advertise in the broadcast media? Maybe. Is it the best place to spend your advertising dollars? Maybe not. If you market your services to consumers or small businesses, broadcast advertising can bring you name recognition with a wide audience. But is there a cheaper way to get the same result?

Go back and reread the introduction to this section, and see if this medium is really worth pursuing. Watch or listen to the stations and shows you might consider as **advertising venues**. Are there any other businesses like yours advertised? If not, there might be a reason.

Especially in radio and television, repeat advertising is the name of the game. Your prospective clients can't tear out your ad and save it, so unless your ad runs constantly, they need to be interested enough in the moment they hear it to write down your phone number or website and remember your name. It's a pretty long shot.

One of the few valid reasons for a professional services business to use broadcast advertising is if your average sale is so low that you need many, many prospects contacting you. In this situation, you might find it necessary to spend more on advertising to get the phone to ring. But be sure to do your math first. No business is profitable unless it earns more per client than it costs to get each one in the door.

To produce an effective radio or TV ad, professional help with your **ad script** and production is mandatory. There's no point in spending big bucks to air a second-rate ad. If the station you plan to advertise with offers to produce your ad for you, survey the quality of other ads it has produced and make sure they meet your standards. As with all other media, track the results of your ads carefully. If you're not getting the results you want, pull the plug.

Chapter 8

Following Up: When You Know Plenty of People but You're Not Contacting Them

"You must do the thing you think you cannot do."
—Eleanor Roosevelt

It's Simple, but Not Always Easy

Doing a good job at follow-up is a piece of cake. You just capture every lead or potential referral partner you run across, then place a call or send them something, or both. If you don't make a sale right away, you put them on the calendar for the next follow-up and do the same thing again. Pretty straightforward, isn't it? So why is follow-up such a problem? Here are the five most common reasons:

1. *Prioritization.* With an activity that you must initiate, it's easy to let other tasks come first: responding to incoming calls and mail, getting the invoices out, going to networking events, and, oh yes, doing the client work you get paid for. If you don't set aside reserved time for follow-up, it will never happen.

2. *Disorganization.* Business cards and scraps of paper lying on your desk do not constitute a contact management system. Without accurate records of the people you have contacted, when, and what your last conversation was about, effective follow-up is impossible.

3. *Lack of Essential Tools.* If you don't know what to say when you call a prospect on the phone, you will probably avoid calling. When you haven't yet created an e-zine, you won't have a reason to ask your

website visitors to provide their e-mail address. Simple follow-up tactics become impossible to implement when you are missing basic components.

4. *Resistance.* Do you find yourself saying, "Why do I have to do this? I'm good at what I do. Why aren't the prospects coming to me?" You are sabotaging yourself with this line of thinking. Business owners much more established than you are doing follow-up every day. It's one of the ways they got established. Regular follow-up does not make people think you don't have enough business; it makes them see you as a professional.

5. *Fear.* "If I follow up that lead, I might be rejected," reasons the voice in your head. "So I'll avoid the pain by not making the call in the first place." Or conversely, you may be thinking, "If I place the call, I might get the business, and then I'll have to do the work, and people will have all these expectations of me." But the reality is that if you don't place the calls, you're going to fail even more dramatically than in these two imaginary scenarios.

By working with the Get Clients Now! system to begin with, you are already addressing three of these issues. Using the 28-day program consistently will help you to set better priorities, overcome resistance, and break through fear. So let's tackle disorganization and some essential follow-up tools next.

Ingredients for Following Up

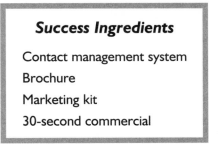

Success Ingredients

Contact management system

Brochure

Marketing kit

30-second commercial

INGREDIENT: *Contact Management System*

Having some kind of **contact management system** is absolutely essential to efficient follow-up. Your chosen method for keeping track of contacts could be a box of 3 x 5-inch cards or a three-ring binder, but most professionals prefer to manage their contacts electronically. Popular choices are desktop computer software like ACT! or Outlook, handheld devices like a Palm or Pocket PC, and smartphones that offer combined contact management, cell phone, and e-mail capabilities.

In addition to recording name, address, phone, fax, and e-mail, the best systems for follow-up allow you also to document the source of each

---

Help, I'm Drowning in Details!

Sylva Leduc is a business and executive coach and the co-founder and former owner of Client Compass, a client information management system for coaches and consultants. Sylva points out: "If you are doing a good job at meeting new people, you'll quickly amass a large number of business cards. It's not too challenging to remember the details about ten or twenty people. If you have a phenomenal memory, you might even recall the specifics about 100 folks you've met. But beyond that, you'd better have a contact management system in place, or you'll soon be drowning in details.

"A simple paper-based system can work for a while, but to be truly efficient and effective, consider one of the many contact management programs available. They save you time; instead of shuffling through piles and files of paper you can instantly put your fingers on information. And contact managers make you look like a *genius* when you remember those tiny little details about someone.

"You can find the best system for your own type of business by conducting an Internet search for 'contact management software' or 'client information management.' Be sure to use quotation marks to keep the search targeted. Then, evaluate some of the many different programs available. If you can find a review from one of the computing magazines, that's even better because they will have done all the research for you. Ask your colleagues for the name of the program they use, their likes and dislikes, how easy it is to use, if training and technical support is available, and the costs.

"Then buy and learn how to use the program. Don't let it sit on your shelf gathering dust. Every time you speak with someone enter notes in your 'virtual filing cabinet.' In short time you'll become trusted as the person who cares enough to remember the details about everyone."

Sylva Leduc, M.Ed., MPEC
www.desktopgoals.com

contact and keep notes about your interaction over time. Handhelds and smartphones can often be synchronized with contact data stored on your desktop or laptop computer to avoid duplication. A contact management system on your office computer will allow you to sort and select contacts by location, original source, date of last contact, or other helpful characteristics. You can use it to print labels, create an e-mail list, or merge personalized information into a boilerplate letter.

Each time you follow up with a contact, or they follow up with you, make a note of when it was, what happened, and when you plan to follow up next. With many systems, once you enter the next follow-up date, you'll receive an automatic reminder when it's due. If your system is paper-based, you should put the next follow-up date in your calendar so you don't forget about it.

If you've been collecting leads for a while before you start using a computerized system, it may seem like an overwhelming task to learn the software and get all your data organized. Just take it a bit at a time. Enter a few names per day and start working with the system slowly. Once you see how much easier an automated system can make your follow-up activities, you'll be motivated to use the system more fully.

INGREDIENT: *Brochure*

The first thing you should consider about creating a **brochure** is whether you need one at all. Many successful consultants, coaches, and professionals never develop a brochure. When they communicate in writing, they rely instead on personal letters and a few supplements, such as a professional biography or résumé and a client list. And professionals often refer prospective clients to their website as an alternative to sending print materials. When you are just starting out, paying for the design and printing of a brochure can be an expensive mistake if the nature of your services, or profile of your target market, is still in flux.

Look at what your successful competitors are doing. If they all seem to have brochures, you may need one also. If they don't, or there seem to be mixed opinions on this subject in your field, ask yourself whether having a brochure will make a positive difference with your prospective clients. If you think it will, how much brochure can you afford?

The simplest and most inexpensive brochure is a standard tri-fold that you or a graphic designer lays out, and prints or photocopies on standard paper stock or preprinted paper designed just for brochures. For marketing personal or household services to consumers, this may be all you need. For business-to-business marketing, a professionally designed and commercially printed brochure will be much more effective. As a general rule, the more expensive your service is, the more expensive your marketing materials should be. Hire a graphic designer, copywriter, or marketing communications specialist to help you, and be sure to work out a budget in advance.

The best way to decide what will go into your brochure is to review many examples of what others have included. Here are some of the typical elements of a tri-fold brochure:

- Attention-getting cover design, perhaps with a logo or photo
- Tag line, positioning statement, or competitive advantage
- Description of the services you offer
- Details about your target market or professional specialty (e.g., "We work with health care companies" or "My specialty is intellectual property law")
- Features and benefits of your services
- Brief biography of you, your company, or both
- Client list, testimonials, or endorsement quotes
- Photographs or illustrations of you or your work
- Address, phone, fax, e-mail, and website

Remember that your brochure should be designed primarily for use in follow-up rather than for filling the pipeline. If you are sending it by mail, it will typically be accompanied by a personal letter or note, and in most other situations, you will be giving your brochure to someone you have had some contact with already. So don't feel your brochure has to communicate everything there is to know about your business. A brochure's best use is to support your marketing activities rather than replacing them.

INGREDIENT: *Marketing Kit*

When marketing to businesses and organizations, a **marketing kit** is more common than a brochure. A typical kit begins with a two-pocket 8 1/2 × 11-inch folder with a cut-out to hold your business card. The contents of your kit are similar to the elements of a tri-fold brochure, with each item laid out on a separate page. Other ingredients might be:

- Fact sheet about your business or your field (e.g., "How to work with an interior designer" or "Our unique approach to team-building")

What's Different About You?

Marketing communications consultant Ellen Looyen has helped thousands of businesses and professionals to brand and package their businesses. Ellen has discovered that, "In a successful marketing piece, everything works together to support the brand identity and message. The copywriting should be persuasive, and the design compelling. An effective brochure needs to exude confidence and convey a sense of quality, honesty, and knowledge to your prospects. It also needs to be written in your prospect's language; generic language is not very effective in the relational marketplace.

"Tell your prospects what you do, how you do it, and who can benefit from what you're offering. It works best to bullet point as much of this information as possible, so readers can scan for what interests them, instead of having to read every word. Be sure to also include a list of several tangible benefits your clients will receive. The most important information in a brochure answers the question, 'What's in it for the client?'

"Endorsements and testimonials work well, because people tend to do what their peers do. Be sure your testimonials point to specific results and are not just fluff. If you can get a testimonial from a well-respected expert in your field, highlight it with a compelling graphic, so it gets the notice it deserves.

"Include a biography that instills confidence in your prospects and brands you as an expert in your field. Tell readers what motivated you to get into this business, and why you are the ideal person to be doing this. Highlight your education, credentials and accomplishments. Give a success story that illustrates the benefits you have achieved for other clients. Make your brochure convey your uniqueness and value with passion, integrity, and believability."

Ellen Looyen
www.ellen4marketing.com

- Articles written by you, about you, or about the kind of work you do
- Testimonial letters from clients
- Case study of a successful project
- Actual samples of work you have produced

A significant advantage of using a kit like this is that you can customize its contents for each recipient. Because you are assembling kits only as you need them, this can be much more affordable than printing several hundred brochures. You can also easily update individual sheets.

Don't overload clients with information, especially on the first contact. Hold back some of what you have, and use it in further follow-up, or as leave-behinds after a presentation.

INGREDIENT: *30-Second Commercial*

When you are calling someone for the first time and get voice mail, use a 30-second commercial to introduce yourself. You may or may not get a return call, but it is a golden opportunity to deliver your marketing message directly into a prospect's ear. A 30-second commercial is also useful in networking situations where you have a chance to stand up and announce to a gathering of interested people more about what you do.

What you don't want to do with your commercial is use it to answer the question, "What do you do?" in conversation. Nor do you want to launch into it when you get a prospect live on the phone. Thirty seconds of you talking without pause is too long for either of those purposes. You can, however, use pieces of your commercial as the basis of an interactive exchange. Developing a strong 30-second commercial will provide you with useful material on which to base a telemarketing call, sales presentation, or conversation with a potential referral partner.

Begin your commercial with your 10-second introduction (see Chapter 7); then continue on with a few details about the services you offer. Always include benefits or results to the client rather than just a list of what you provide. Here are two examples:

"My name is Chris Winston. I help human resource departments keep track of employees, salaries, and benefits. I'm an HR information systems consultant. If your current system isn't keeping up with your needs, I can fix inaccurate reports, install software upgrades, help you meet regulatory requirements, and make the system easier to use. When your system needs replacing, I'll make sure you avoid expensive mistakes, and work with your staff step-by-step to manage a system replacement on time and under budget. Since I specialize in HR, you can be sure I understand all of your unique needs, and stay current on what's essential for you to know."

"I'm Mai Nguyen, and I help my clients maintain healthy lifestyles despite daily stress and chronic medical conditions. I'm a lifestyle coach. If you or your patients are suffering from stress, overwork, or ongoing health problems, I can help with choosing a healthy diet, developing an exercise program, and applying stress management techniques to support increased wellness. I work with individuals and health practitioners to make sure people with health challenges don't just talk about lifestyle changes, they make them. I'm a stress management instructor and certified fitness counselor, so you can be confident that I have the training and experience to help my clients live healthier lives."

 Strategy: Direct Contact and Follow-Up

and

 **Networking and Referral Building**

> ### *Success Ingredients*
>
> Model marketing letter
>
> In-house mailing list
>
> Postcard or mailer
>
> Newsletter or e-zine
>
> E-mail autoresponders
>
> Personal connections

In the follow-up stage of marketing, you are using only two strategies: (1) direct contact and follow-up, and (2) networking and referral building. It's important to notice that the activities involved in pursuing these two different strategies are identical: calling and mailing, follow-up meetings, follow-up mailings, and following up on the Web. The difference is in the targets of these activities. Direct contact and follow-up is aimed at prospects, and networking and referral building can be aimed at either prospects or referral partners.

In professions where directly soliciting business is inappropriate, you may be using the strategies in this chapter more for networking to increase referrals than for making contact with prospects. Nevertheless, don't neglect to follow up with prospects as much as you can without crossing the line. Sending a nice-to-meet-you note, interesting article, or informational newsletter is always appropriate, whether you are selling to organizations or to individuals.

RECIPE: *Calling and Mailing*

When you are contacting someone for the first time, whether it is a potential client or a possible referral partner, the most effective approach is to call, mail, and call, as described in Chapter 7. In other words, call before you mail or e-mail, and call again after you mail.

If you find you are talking to someone both interested and qualified (for example, able to pay), you may be able to arrange a presentation or a networking meeting on your first call. It's more likely, though, you will reach voice mail, an assistant, or someone with "no time to talk." This is why being organized and persistent about follow-up is so important. Once you have made an initial contact, even if only through voice mail or a receptionist, you must follow up with a postal mailing, another call, an e-mail, or even stopping by—and you will probably have to do this more than once.

Never assume that someone you are calling is going to call you back. Often, they won't. Busy people simply don't have the time to return unsolicited phone calls or, in fact, any call that isn't their top priority that day. If you are of the opinion that not returning a phone call is rude, get over it. Even people you are in the final stages of negotiating a sale with will often not return calls for days or weeks. If you are willing to accept this as a normal business practice, your marketing life will be much less stressful.

It's not a good idea to rely on e-mail as your only method of follow-up communication. For one thing, it's too easy to hide behind—for both you and your prospects. You will find that interactive conversations will be much more productive in determining people's interest level in your offer and handling any objections they have to meeting or working with you. Unless you are absolutely sure that e-mail is the preferred method of communication for a particular prospect, alternate your e-mails with phone calls.

Also, don't make the assumption that just because you sent an e-mail it was either received or read. E-mail addresses change, e-mails get lost in transmission, mail filters block them, and some people receive far too many e-mails to ever read them all.

When sending postal mail or e-mail to someone you have not yet spoken to, keep it simple. Until you know whether the person is interested, don't mail more than a personal letter with a brochure or fact sheet enclosed. If you are e-mailing, reference your website, but don't send any attached files. On the other hand, if your initial conversation with this person prompted interest, but not an appointment for a meeting or discussion, you may wish to send more information now in the hope of convincing him to meet with you. If you use a marketing kit, this is typically when you would send it.

To make this process easier, it is helpful to have a **model marketing letter**, a standard letter that you can personalize to fit a specific situation. Your letter's first paragraphs typically introduce you or your company, but that shouldn't be your opening line. The best lead sentence will be one that establishes a **personal connection** between you and the recipient. For example: "I heard you speak at the Iowa Manufacturer's conference," "Rafael Santos suggested I contact you," or "I'm a fellow member of the Northside Community Alliance."

When writing to a prospect with whom you have no connection, a good second choice can be to lead with an attention-getting question, such as "Would you like to increase sales by 30 percent this year?" or "Is your relocation company meeting your needs?" Keep the tone of your letter helpful, informative, and professional. Avoid overly promotional copy and hard-sell techniques. Remember that this is a personal letter from you to someone you want to build a relationship with. It's not a direct mail piece aimed at an anonymous buyer.

Next, highlight the benefits of what you offer. Don't just repeat what is in your brochure; expand on it or talk about some actual client results. If you have enough information to do so, suggest specifically how you can help the prospect you are writing to by describing a problem or goal that person has and your proposed solution. Then, describe briefly what qualifies you to provide the service you are offering.

You might create a model letter for each different service that you offer, or one for prospects and another for referral partners. One to one-and-a-half pages is a good length. Once you have created a model, all you will have to customize each time is the opening sentence where you state your connection, plus any specific offer of help. See Figures 8-1 and 8-2 for some examples.

Figure 8-1 Model Marketing Letter—Warm Contact

Dear Johnny,

It was great to chat with you at the RTIR seminar. You mentioned that you're interested in learning more about my marketing services, so here is some information about how I work.

I create marketing strategies and write news releases and other promotional materials for many clients in the publishing industry.

Book press releases are a specialty of mine; I aim to do right by your book without charging a fortune. I also evaluate marketing materials, including websites, for their effectiveness. My clients have included publishers and authors in just about every genre (fiction, nonfiction, how-to, children's, even poetry).

I look for "the story behind the story." Publishing a book is not in itself a news event—it happens 190,000 times a year, just in the U.S. So, for a nonfiction title, I look at how it helps the reader solve a problem, gain new in-sight, or achieve success. For a fiction title, I may choose to tie it to real-world events, I may call attention to the book's literary quality . . . I will use the strategy that most suits the book and the market.

As an example, I was hired to write a press release for a new book on electronic privacy. Instead of the boring, ex-pected "Electronic Privacy Expert Releases New Book," my headline was "It's 10 O'Clock—Do You Know Where Your Credit History Is?" Another publisher did a side-by-side test, sending out my press release to half his list, and his own release to the other half. He reported that my release had generated six times the response of his own, and has now been using my services regularly for several years.

I'll be happy to help you with . . .

Press Releases and PSAs	Catalog and Ad Copy
Brochures	Direct Mail Sales Letters
Press Kits	Jacket and Cover Copy
Backgrounders	Marketing Strategies
Fliers	

I am the author of six books, including the award-winning *Grassroots Marketing: Getting Noticed in a Noisy World*. I've been writing marketing materials and developing strate-gies focused on affordable, effective approaches since 1974.

Let's talk soon. I look forward to working with you.

Warmly,

Shel Horowitz

www.frugalmarketing.com

Figure 8-2 Model Marketing Letter—Cold Contact

Dear Consuela:

I'm a fellow member of the Women in Business Net-work, and I saw your catering business listed in our directory. Are you looking for more clients right now? I help women business owners and self-employed professionals build their client base quickly without spending all their time at work. I'm a business and personal coach.

Many of my clients find that working with me has doubled their bottom line in a relatively short time. We focus together on identifying practical, affordable business-building strategies that fit your professional image and personal style. I've helped other women in the catering business land more clients and bigger jobs without increasing their advertising budget or working longer hours.

I can assist you with business planning, marketing strategy, time management issues, and balancing work with your personal life, all at a rate you can afford.

I've been doing this work since 2003 and have a number of references I could share with you. I teach marketing at the Hilltop Career Center and write articles on entrepreneurship for their newsletter.

I look forward to finding out if I could be of service to you, and I'll give you a call next week.

Regards,

Tomiko Mifune

(732) 555-1212

A week to ten days after sending your information, place a follow-up call. Don't make the mistake of thinking that if your prospects were truly interested, they would call you. Think about how many days or weeks a low-priority task can languish on your own to-do list. When you get a prospect on the phone, try again for a presentation. If it doesn't happen this time either, ask if you can follow up at some later date, and determine what an appropriate interval would be: next month, next quarter, or even next year. Then make the entry in your contact management system and move on to the next prospect.

What if you keep getting voice mail? While it is true that some people let all their calls roll to voice mail, you can sometimes get through to a business prospect by calling off hours, say before 8:30 or after 5:30. You may also find people at their desks during the lunch hour. When calling individuals at home, early evening or Saturday is often the best time. But should you keep calling or leave a message? Actually, you should do both. Since you are assuming that most people won't call you back, keep right on calling them.

Whether you reach your contacts or not, never make them feel wrong for not returning your calls. Rather than saying a bit peevishly, "I haven't heard from you," instead let them know you are eager to speak with them and wanted to try again while you were in your office. As a general rule, leaving three voice mail messages over a ten-day period of time is sufficient. If you get no response, wait a month and try again.

When you do leave a message, use your 30-second commercial on the first call. In later messages, leave a new and interesting piece of information each time. When calling a prospect, make it a benefit of doing business with you, for example, "I can help you save up to 20 percent on your training costs." Keep your messages to no more than 30 seconds; no one likes to receive lengthy voice mails, and the delete key is at their fingertips.

If you have called, left messages, and still can't get through to the person you want, send a follow-up e-mail. Many people will quickly respond to e-mail because it is easy. If you can interest them in what you have to offer, they may be willing to set up a phone appointment with you to discuss it further.

If you are new at persistent follow-up, it's likely that at some point you will begin to feel you are pestering people. Keep in mind that you have much more awareness about these calls and messages than the person receiving them does. Part of the reason you need to keep contacting people is that they will often forget about you almost immediately. Be pleasant, helpful, and upbeat in your messages, and most recipients will respect your professionalism. If a prospect really doesn't want to hear from you again, he or she will tell you so, usually quite politely.

So when should you give up on contacting a prospect? That depends on the value of the potential sale. A $1,000 sale might only be worth five attempts by letter, call, or e-mail, but a $10,000 sale would certainly pay for many more. Every salesperson has a story about a client who finally said yes after the seventeenth phone call, so if the sale seems worth it, don't quit.

RECIPE: *Follow-Up Meetings*

Your first live meeting with a prospect after your initial contact is typically some sort of presentation, whether it takes place in person or by phone. Even if this is primarily a fact-finding meeting, you will be spending some time talking about your services and qualifications. If a second meeting is necessary, it might be a formal presentation to a larger group, an informal meeting where you discuss a proposal you have prepared, or simply a conversation about the details of the proposed work. After this, you may find yourself following up mostly by phone messages, e-mail, letter, or fax. The same is also true for referral partners. After an initial meeting in person or by phone, you might not speak to them again in person.

When following up over a long period of time, try to find ways to connect with your contacts or prospects person to person to keep the relationship alive. If they live or work near you, take them to lunch, meet for coffee, stop by their offices (if this would be appropriate), or seek them out at networking events. For those not in your area, make an appointment for a phone conversation to talk about their current needs, new projects, personal news, or other topics you have in common. You'll find that a periodic live conversation will keep their awareness of your name and business high, and will ultimately result in more referrals and more sales.

RECIPE: *Follow-Up Mailings*

Whenever you meet someone at a networking event who is not an immediate prospect, an easy and inexpensive way to follow up immediately is to send a nice-to-meet-you note. Depending on the nature of the contact, you might include an interesting article or your brochure or fact sheet. Then add the person to your contact management system for later follow-up.

As you work to fill the pipeline, you will constantly be collecting names and addresses for your **in-house mailing list**. If you enter the ones you want to keep into your contact management system as you collect them, eventually you will have a substantial list. When your list reaches about 300 names, it's probably time to start thinking about sending your list some kind of mail or e-mail on a regular basis. This mail to your in-house list is for the purpose of following up with people you already know to remind them of your services and continue building your relationship with them. It's very different from direct mail or bulk e-mail sent to strangers on a prospect list that you bought or compiled.

The Power of Postcards

Roger C. Parker is the author of 35 books on marketing and design, including the perennial bestseller *Looking Good in Print* (Coriolis, 1998). Roger advises, "If you're not presently using postcards to promote your business, you're missing out on a lot of potential profits. Postcards are effective, easy to produce, and inexpensive to print and mail.

"Think of postcards as 'billboards you can mail.' Just as it's hard to ignore billboards while driving, your clients and prospects will find it difficult to ignore your message when they encounter it on a postcard in their mailbox. A brightly colored postcard sent via conventional mail will often attract more attention than the same message sent via e-mail.

"You can prepare the artwork for a postcard in minutes with programs like Microsoft Publisher. Then you can print them one at a time or in small batches on your black and white or color inkjet printer. You can use local commercial printers to print larger quantities, or order four-color postcards at extremely low prices from a mail order specialty printer.

"It's also possible now to use your computer to send personalized color postcards in quantities of 1 to 1,000 from a print-on-demand postcard service. You can design, write, and address your postcards completely online, and your postcards will be printed and mailed first class from a centralized location the next business day.

"In postcard design, the simpler your message, and the larger the type, the more likely it will be read. Use color with care. Type reversed out of a colored background is more effective than setting type in color. Maintain consistency by using the same color, typeface, and logo used on your business cards, letterheads, and newsletters. Also, two postcards will generate far more results than a single mailing. Schedule a follow-up postcard to arrive soon after your first."

Roger C. Parker
www.onepagenewsletters.com

As a rule, sending a general mailing a minimum of four times per year is sufficient to keep your name visible to your prospects and referral partners. With hot prospects or frequent referrers, you will probably want to be in contact more often than this. In addition to phone calls or meetings, you might send these special people personal notes by mail or e-mail, along with articles of interest, links to useful websites, or invitations to upcoming events.

For your general mailing, you could opt for a simple piece like a **postcard or mailer**, or put more effort into publishing your own **newsletter or e-zine**. Postcards, self-mailers, and other small pieces sent by postal mail typically take the form of reminders or seasonal announcements with an attention-getting tag line and graphic. Here are some examples:

Overloaded with year-end work? Time to call Design Solutions.

Sales in a slump? Take Charge Marketing can help.

January special—25% off your first appointment!

Keep the amount of text to a minimum. A mailer is not intended to do the job of a brochure. What you want is for the recipients to contact you with their questions, not get all the information they need from your mailer.

Producing a print **newsletter** can be a sizeable job, requiring skills on several levels: how-to writing for articles, copywriting for promotional sections, and graphic design for art and layout. If your skills in these areas are limited, get some professional help, especially with design. Homemade newsletters usually look it, and there's no point putting in this much time and money if your prospects won't be impressed.

A print newsletter can be as few as two pages or as many as eight. Typical contents include one or more informative articles aimed at your market niche, interspersed with several shorter items sharing news, resources, or inspiration. Be sure your newsletter contains more useful information than it does promotional copy. Ideally, you want the people on your mailing list not only to read your newsletter but to pass it along to friends as a helpful resource.

Instead of a print newsletter, you might choose to use an e-zine, and there's more about that in the next section. But despite its higher expense, a print newsletter can be an effective choice with prospects who will pay more attention to postal mail than to e-mail. This can include both people who don't use e-mail much and those who get far too much e-mail already. A print newsletter can also be used as a marketing piece that you distribute at workshops or networking events, hand out at trade shows, or include in your marketing kit.

RECIPE: *Following Up on the Web*

One of the most powerful ways to follow up with prospects on the Internet is to publish a regular **e-zine** or electronic newsletter. Most e-zines are delivered by e-mail, although some are made available only on the Web. An e-zine can be much more affordable than a print newsletter because there is no printing or postage to pay for, and typically less design work. If you plan at the outset to collect e-mail addresses from all your prospects, you'll be able to use your in-house mailing list to send your e-zine to hundreds or thousands of prospects with a single click.

The most popular e-zine format is a monthly e-mail publication that mimics the contents of a typical print newsletter, including an article or two, some promotional copy, and perhaps two or three shorter items. But many other formats are possible. You can send an e-zine quarterly, weekly, or even daily. Instead of articles, your e-zine can consist of brief tips, either one tip per issue or a collection of tips each time. Subscribe to some other e-zines published in your market niche and see what formats appeal to you and are a good match for your professional image, personal style, and the time you have available to commit to publication.

Another variety of e-zine is to publish a blog (discussed in Chapter 7) and provide a way for readers to receive your blog posts by e-mail. When prospects visit your blog on the Web, they can subscribe themselves to your e-mail list using an automated service, or you can ask members of your existing in-house list if they would like to receive e-mailed posts from your new blog.

An alternative to e-mail delivery for either blogs or e-zines is to give readers the option to subscribe using a newsreader (e.g., Google Reader or a My Yahoo! page). You can set up an automated feed of your blog posts or e-zine issues that subscribers can view using the newsreader of their choice, along with other blogs, e-zines, and news items they read regularly.

There are a wide variety of technologies to choose from for creating and distributing an e-zine by e-mail. Instead of sending your e-zine to subscribers the same way you currently send personal e-mail, you will probably want to use an automated system to deliver your e-zine and maintain your mailing list. These systems allow your website visitors to

You'll Sell More if You Don't Sell Anything

"An e-newsletter is the next best thing to having lunch with every one of your clients and prospects once each month," declares Michael Katz, author of *E-Newsletters That Work* (Xlibris, 2003). "But what do you think would happen if every time you got together for lunch, you tried to sell those people something? My guess is they would stop having lunch with you.

"The reason I bring up this lunchtime scenario is that when it comes to how you develop and manage your e-newsletter, there are a number of similarities. Your e-newsletter functions as kind of an electronic proxy for all those face-to-face interactions that can't possibly happen in the physical world. It puts you in front of your target audience on a regular schedule, and in a nonthreatening context.

"There are tangible, measurable, undeniable business benefits associated with relationship building. All those lunches, as nonlinear and unstructured as they may be, have results. But focusing on the desired result (i.e., more sales), at the expense of the relationship, eliminates both. If you use a relationship-building opportunity to make a sales pitch, not only do you eat a lot of lunches by yourself, you also eliminate one of the easiest, most efficient means for growing your business. It's certainly fine to talk about what you do, but you can't make it the center of the conversation. As far as your e-newsletter goes, if it becomes nothing more than a telemarketing call in disguise, people will unsubscribe, putting an end to both the conversation and any related future opportunities.

"Effective e-newsletters require that you turn the selling machine off. Like a cherished lunchtime companion, a good e-newsletter focuses on offering relevant, useful, interesting information to readers, with an emphasis on providing—not extracting—value."

Michael Katz
www.bluepenguindevelopment.com

add themselves to your mailing list, update their own e-mail address when it changes, and unsubscribe themselves automatically if they wish. If you search the Web for "e-zine publishing," "e-mail marketing," or "e-mail autoresponders," you'll find many systems available to choose from, a host of helpful articles on producing an e-zine, and a variety of vendors who can help you with the process.

You should never subscribe someone to your e-zine without his or her permission. First, an e-zine is most appropriately used as a relationship-building follow-up tool, not as a vehicle for filling the pipeline. The people you send your e-zine to should already know who you are. Second, the sending of unsolicited bulk e-mail is governed by a wide variety of government regulations, most of which can be translated as "don't send bulk e-mail to people who haven't asked for it." Third, subscribing your prospects to an e-mail publication that they never asked for and have expressed no interest in is more likely to be considered an annoyance than a courtesy.

A much better approach to gaining subscribers is to routinely ask clients and prospects if they would like to subscribe to your e-zine when you first make contact with them. When you publish your first issue, most people on your existing in-house list will not be offended if you send a complimentary copy asking if they would like to become subscribers. But don't subscribe them first, and ask them to unsubscribe if they don't want it.

One more method of following up on the Web is using **e-mail autoresponders** to send information or a series of informational messages to people who inquire about your services. Autoresponder systems send prewritten e-mail messages automatically, and are available from many of the same vendors who provide e-zine distribution. The most common use of an autoresponder is to provide an instant reply to someone who requests more information while visiting your website. The advantage of using an autoresponder instead of displaying the same details on your site is that once someone makes a request via autoresponder, you have her e-mail address and can follow up with her later.

The same autoresponder that provides an immediate reply to an inquiry like this can also be used to send a series of messages at pretimed intervals after the initial inquiry. For example, if a prospective home buyer makes a request on a real estate agent's site for additional details about some current listings, an autoresponder could send her three more messages after seven, fourteen, and thirty days, each one offering a new tip about home buying and another reason to choose that agent to help with her home purchase.

It's a good idea to include a notice at the beginning of the series that lets prospects know you'll be sending additional informational messages, and gives them a chance to unsubscribe immediately if they don't wish to receive them. That way your prospects will be "opting in" to the series and you won't offend anyone. You can use the same list later on to broadcast occasional messages to subscribers after your preprogrammed series ends. Just as with an e-zine, you'll find that messages with useful content for readers will keep subscribers longer than those that simply deliver marketing messages.

RECIPE: *Strengthening Personal Connections*

One of the biggest challenges during the follow-up stage of the Universal Marketing Cycle is getting people to respond to your calls and e-mails. When prospects enter your marketing pipeline as a result of your cold call, their casual visit to your website, or your finding their name on a list, you are essentially a stranger. Unless they have a compelling need for the service you are offering at the exact moment you contact them, they have no real incentive to take your call or answer your e-mail.

You can't make a prospect need you. But what you can do is identify and strengthen the **personal connections** you have with your prospects to increase the likelihood that they will be open to speaking with you.

When you have a particular prospect you can't seem to get through to, one useful tactic is to ask for an introduction from someone you already know. Ask your colleagues, others in your market niche, or members of the business and personal networks you belong to if they know this person. If so, would they be willing to serve as your connection? You might request that your connection call or e-mail your prospect suggesting he speak with you, or simply ask if you can use your connection's name as someone who referred you.

A more helpful approach overall, though, is to focus on filling your marketing pipeline with prospects you are already connected to in the first place. The people you are personally acquainted with in your market niche will probably already be on your prospect list. But your personal connections go far beyond those people you have actually met. Here are some suggestions for people you have a connection with that may not have occurred to you:

- Members of any association, club, affinity group, or online community you belong to

Find a Fix for Your Discomfort

"The Discomfort Dilemma is that perilous moment when you stand poised between doing whatever is the next step in the selling process—or doing something to avoid it," describes Carol Costello, author of *The Soul of Selling* (Benbella, 2005). "That next step might be making a cold call, calling back the person you agreed to call last week, promising results, or anything that involves discomfort, the possibility of failure, or any potential for rejection.

"In the midst of the Discomfort Dilemma, almost anywhere seems better than where you are. And there are so many more comfortable things to do! You could call a friend. You need to keep up those relationships, after all. You could play with the cat. The poor thing needs exercise. You could e-mail your aunt, or even pay the bills. Hey, you could shampoo the rug!

"Bills do need to be paid. Rugs need to be shampooed. *But not during the time when you said you'd make calls.*

"For each of your own most likely Discomfort Dilemmas, you need to devise a fix that gets you moving past that paralyzing moment of indecision and takes you into action. One of my clients hated to make the first call of the day. Her fix was to spend a moment before she picked up the phone remembering a recent call that had been particularly pleasant. Another client's Dilemma was that when things were going well and she was ahead of the game, she felt an irresistible desire to shop. She learned to say to herself, 'Just do what you promised yourself. When you've done it, you can spend the whole rest of the month in the stores if you want.'

"Be imaginative. One client got a tube of glitter glue, and saved it for Discomfort Dilemmas. When she completed the task she had been resisting, she ran a line of glue over it on her to-do list. That may sound strange, but when it comes to the Discomfort Dilemma, you want whatever gets you through the night. That woman made more than $350,000 last year, and I, for one, don't laugh at her glitter glue."

Carol Costello
www.soulofselling.com

- Other employees of any company you have worked for (as an employee or consultant)
- Vendors or salespeople who serve your current clients
- Alumni and faculty of any university or training school you went to
- Speakers at any meeting or conference you attended
- Parents of other children at the schools your children attend
- Current and former co-workers of your family members and close friends
- Your neighbors and neighborhood merchants
- Your local political representatives

When you look at how many names could be added to your prospect list from these sources, your circle of connections is probably much more extensive than you thought. Consider approaching prospects who fall into any of these categories instead of those with whom you can't find a connection. When writing a letter or placing a call, name the specific connection you have with each prospect in your opening. You may be surprised to see how many more people will start taking your calls.

Another Word About Fear

The thought of making follow-up calls may be even more paralyzing than cold calling. After all, this is someone you already believe needs your services. Maybe you've already talked or sent your literature. You've invested something or made a personal connection, so now if you hear no, the rejection really feels personal.

What you have to remember is that rejection is not about you. This is a business transaction. Your prospect is deciding whether or not to spend his own or the company's money. The number of factors that go into a decision like this are innumerable. And frequently, what you are told about why the prospect doesn't want to go forward isn't the full story. Here are some actual reasons that people with a strong need for the service being offered have decided not to buy or have bought from a competitor:

What you were told. . . .	*What's really going on. . . .*
It's too expensive.	I decided to take a Hawaiian vacation instead.
We don't think you're right for the job.	We got a competing bid from my cousin's boyfriend.
I changed my mind.	I'm getting a divorce and can't think about anything else now.
We have other priorities right now.	The company is going bankrupt.
I can't afford it.	I don't want to take money out of a mutual fund to pay for it.
We're not ready to make a change.	My boss doesn't want headquarters to know there's a problem.
We found someone more qualified.	We liked the competitor's tag line.
Don't call us; we'll call you.	The project was tabled until next year.

When a prospect tells you a competitor was chosen because he or she "has more experience," the message is that the company hires only people with strong experience in its own industry. This is not about you. If you are told the competition "came well recommended," the prospect is choosing to do business with the friend of a friend. It's not about you. When you hear that the other guy's bid was lower, it means the buyer values price over quality. Also, not about you.

The real trick to vanquishing fear of follow-up is to have so many prospects in the pipeline that any one "no" becomes much less important.

Chapter 9

Getting Presentations: When You're Contacting People but Not Getting Appointments

"Consider the postage stamp . . . It secures success through its ability to stick to one thing until it gets there."
— Josh Billings, nineteenth-century Yankee humorist

What's in the Way?

At this stage in the Universal Marketing Cycle, you are more than halfway home. With a full pipeline and consistent follow-up, you are bound to make plenty of sales, right? Well, usually that's true. Finding the right people to talk to, and actually talking to them, will produce results in most cases. But sometimes, it's not quite enough.

A presentation, whether it takes place in person, by phone, or even by e-mail, is a conversation you have with a prospect to find out what he needs and describe to him what you can do. It's a necessary step in almost every sale of professional services. If you're not presenting, it's pretty likely that you're not getting clients.

When you find yourself making lots of contacts but rarely getting to make a presentation, there's something in the way. Assuming that you have a service your target market needs in the first place, and it's priced within the range your market can pay, what else might be preventing people from wanting to hear what you have to offer? Here are some possibilities:

1. *You're not using the right words.* When you send a letter or call on the phone, or prospects call you or visit your website, they aren't understanding how you can help them.

2. *Your telemarketing skills aren't up to the task.* You are nervous or unprepared when you get on the phone, and aren't able to engage people in conversation.

3. *The prospects you are talking to aren't qualified enough.* They don't have a need, can't pay, or are otherwise not ready to take action.

4. *You aren't well-known enough, or haven't been recommended,* so prospects are hesitant to take their time to talk with you.

5. *Your competition seems to have the market locked up.* No one wants to talk to you because they're already being served by someone else.

6. *You are offering what you think your prospects need instead of what they think they need.* They don't see how your service fits into their plans.

7. *The way your services are packaged doesn't make sense to your prospects.* For example, they want to pay a flat fee, and you are charging by the hour.

8. *You are offering so many services that your prospects can't quite figure out what you actually do* and how it matches up with their needs.

In the next two sections, you will find solutions to many of these problems. Suggestions for doing a better job at making contact with your prospects appear first, followed by some ideas for improving your strategic market position.

 Strategy: Direct Contact and Follow-Up

> ### Success Ingredients
>
> Telemarketing script/skills
> Qualifying questions
> Higher quality leads and referrals
> "Stickier" website

RECIPE: *Making the Pitch*

One of the quickest fixes to your personal marketing approach can be to change the words you use. An effective **telemarketing script** positions what you are offering in such a way that prospects grasp what's in it for them. A common mistake is to call prospects with the intent of introducing yourself and telling them what you do. But that's all about you. Why should they care?

Instead, introduce yourself by giving simply your name and any personal connection between you. Then immediately ask about them. "Do you have a moment to talk about your concerns with the reliability of your network?" is a sample opening question. Try leading with a benefit: "I help companies increase employee retention without added costs. Is employee turnover a problem you're concerned about?" Or ask a qualifying question as your first step: "Are you looking for a new job opportunity right now?"

This is also what you should do when prospects call you. Before launching into a description of how you work and what it costs, ask about their situation.

Engaging your prospects in conversation will both establish rapport and provide you with valuable information. Whenever you can, ask open-ended questions rather than encouraging yes or no answers. "How much use do you expect to make of outside trainers this year?" can get you much more information than asking, "Does your company use contract trainers?" Include a series of possible questions like this in your script.

The word "script" is not meant to imply that you are reading something prepared. You don't want to come off as if you are selling newspaper subscriptions. Design your script as a list of talking points that you refer to as needed during an interactive conversation.

When you feel that you have both established rapport and collected enough information from your prospects, tell them briefly and specifically how you can help them, and in their words. If the prospect says "our employee turnover is out of control," you might respond with, "I can really help you with that out-of-control turnover situation. The incentive plan I implemented for Althea Chemical reduced their turnover by 20 percent."

As soon as you know you've got the person's interest, ask for a meeting or turn the call into an immediate phone presentation. Don't wait for her to suggest the next step or back away from making it a direct question. "It sounds as if my services might be just what you're looking for. Would you like to get together and talk about it?" Expect to encounter objections, and have a ready answer for each predictable stumbling block already in your script.

If you have trouble remembering what's in your script, get nervous once you're on the phone, or just can't seem to think quickly enough to deliver the right responses, you need to work on your **telemarketing skills**. Take a class, work with a coach, or practice with friends. Learning your script more thoroughly will enable you to give a better performance under stress.

Prospects Are Also People

"Treat the person you contact like a human being, not a prospect," recommends Jill Konrath, author of *Selling to Big Companies* (Kaplan, 2005). "In calling a friend, you'd automatically ask if you were interrupting: 'Is it a bad time?' You would notice if they sounded distracted and address it head on: 'Hey, if you're swamped right now, I don't want to interrupt. I'd rather catch you when you have a few minutes to talk.' And you'd immediately suggest a future contact: 'When is a good time to call you back?'

"Prepare for the common obstacles prior to the call—and eliminate them if at all possible. For example, they say, 'We already use XYZ.' You respond: 'Well I assume a company of your size would be working with another firm. (pause) *And* that's why we need to meet . . .'

"Or they say, 'We're really busy right now. We couldn't possibly take time to look at options.' You respond: 'You and I know that six months from now your workload isn't going to be any lighter. *And* that's exactly why we need to get together . . .'

"Please note that the second sentence in these examples starts with *and*, not *but*! Because the 'and' doesn't negate your prospect's perspective, they will be interested in learning more.

"Then, reel off two to three valid business reasons that this prospect should get together with you. They need to flow out of your mouth without hesitation, so prepare them ahead of time. These are true statements, not slippery manipulations, so make sure you state them with quiet confidence.

"Sounding like a sleazy, well-oiled seller will not get you an appointment in today's market. Think of your phone calls as business-to-business conversations with peers. That may be a hard mind shift to make, but it's where you need to be."

Jill Konrath
www.sellingtobigcompanies.com

RECIPE: *Qualifying Your Prospects*

One of the barriers to landing presentations is pursuing the wrong prospects. You may have done a good job at defining your target market, but not everyone in your market needs your service now or can afford to pay. **Qualifying questions** are intended to determine whether a prospect is hot, warm, or cold, so you can gauge your level of effort accordingly. Typical qualifiers are:

- Asking if they have a particular problem your service solves or a goal it aids
- Finding out how much they are expecting to pay or have paid in the past
- Determining if they have a budget set aside for the work
- Asking how soon they are expecting to get started or have the project completed
- Knowing if the person you are talking to is the decision-maker

When you speak to a prospect by phone or in person, you can ask questions like these directly. If you receive inquiries by e-mail, encourage prospects to tell you more when they write. The "contact us" page on your website might suggest a few questions you'd like them to answer, or you can provide a contact form for them to complete.

If you find that once you start asking these questions, your prospect list starts looking pretty chilly, you need some **higher-quality leads and referrals.** What is the profile of the client most likely to buy? Where can you get more leads that fit that profile? If you don't know the answers to these questions, you may need to do more research on your target market. (See the next section for some suggestions.)

Another solution is getting more referral-based leads, rather than working from prospect lists or relying on tips from your networking contacts. A client who is personally referred to you by someone they trust will almost always move forward to the presentation stage immediately, because they have prequalified *you*.

RECIPE: *Making Your Website "Stickier"*

An ongoing challenge with marketing professional services on the Web is your lack of personal, ongoing contact with visitors to your website. If a prospect only visits your site once and never gets past glancing at your home page, it has no more impact than seeing a one-time ad for your ser-

---

If You Don't Ask, You're Selling in the Dark

Josiane Feigon teaches people who sell by phone to use her TeleSmart Qualification Criteria to determine if the people they are speaking to will be worth pursuing as potential buyers. Here are some of the areas that Josiane suggests you focus on:

"Business Needs—What are your short- and long-term goals? What is driving your interest in this solution? What capabilities are you looking for?

"Decision-Making Responsibility—What is your role in the decision-making process? What other groups will be involved in decision making? Who will be involved in evaluation on the business side? On the technical side?

"Decision-Making Criteria—What will you base the decision on? What information do you need to make your decision? What is important to you in a vendor?

"Competition—Where are you in your research process? What other vendor solutions do you have in-house? What other solutions have you looked at?

"Time Frame—When would you like to be up and running? Walk me through your timeline from research to implementation. When will you be ready to review a proposal?

"Budget—How much money do you have set aside for this project? What type of budget items have been approved?"

Josiane Feigon
www.tele-smart.com

---

vice in a magazine. In order to convert site visitors into interested prospects who are open to a conversation about what you can do for them, you need to keep them on your site longer, encourage them to return for future visits, and provide a vehicle for following up with them over time. What you need is a **"stickier" website**.

Making your website stickier can involve any or all of three different approaches:

Provide useful information that first-time visitors will want to explore. This will begin to build the know, like, and trust factor and increase the likelihood that they will inquire about working with you. Helpful articles, case studies, and facts about your profession will keep them on your site longer and reading more.

Offer interactive tools that people will return to your site to use again. Add assessments or quizzes, a message board, an event calendar, or tutorials that showcase your expertise. If your site has a blog, add a commenting feature to encourage interaction. Updating the resources on your site frequently will encourage repeat visits.

Capture the e-mail address of your visitors by offering them an e-zine or blog subscription or a free report, audio download, or mini-course delivered by e-mail. This will enable you to follow up with them to provide additional information and determine their level of interest in working with you.

Actively maintaining a website with many different features can be a huge undertaking. Be careful that you are not investing more time and money in your Web presence than the resulting sales are worth. Remember to ask yourself the essential question needed to evaluate any marketing tactic—is there a cheaper and easier way you could generate the same amount of revenue?

 Strategy: Networking and Referral Building,

 Public Speaking,

 Writing and Publicity,

and

 Promotional Events

> ### *Success Ingredients*
>
> Professional visibility
> Competitive research
> Target market research
> New market position
> Better service package
> Narrower focus of services

RECIPE: *Getting More Visible*

If the first time that prospective clients hear your name is when you call them to make an appointment, you will find it much harder to get their attention than if they already know you or know of you. Increasing your **professional visibility** is not just a tactic for filling the pipeline; it's also a way to influence buying decisions.

Networking and referral building activities will help you become more visible in your market niche. Attend networking events frequented by your clients and prospects. Volunteer in a high-profile position, such as the program committee of an association your clients belong to, or as chairperson of a project likely to get good coverage in the trade press. The strategies of writing and publicity and public speaking will help you to become more visible professionally, while simultaneously building your credibility. Promotional events like free teleclasses, workshops, or

---

Connecting with the Invisible

"Products are made; services are *delivered*," asserts Harry Beckwith, author of *Selling the Invisible* (Warner, 1997), *The Invisible Touch* (Warner, 2000), and *What Clients Love* (Warner, 2003). "Products are used; services are *experienced*. Products possess physical characteristics we can evaluate before we buy; services *do not even exist before we buy* them. We request them, often paying in advance. Then we receive them.

"And finally, products are impersonal: bricks, mortar, pens, car seats, fruit—things with no human connection to us. Services, by contrast, are *personal*—often frighteningly so. A service relationship touches our essence and reveals the people involved: provider and customer. For that reason, a service marketing course belongs in the school of the humanities. Service marketers, like humanities scholars, strive to answer this question: 'What does it mean to be a human being?'

". . . Our lives seem increasingly disconnected. Our grown children move farther from home; technology reduces direct contact with people. Our drive for connection grows more intense. Making genuine, human connections becomes more important everywhere—not least of all in our businesses every day."

Harry Beckwith
www.beckwithpartners.com

demonstrations give you a reason to send out invitations and press releases and increase your exposure.

All of these strategies have a higher effectiveness rating than advertising in bringing you more visibility with your target audience. They will allow you to establish the personal connections and trust that result in landing more presentations and easier sales.

RECIPE: *Evaluating Your Market Position*

The position that you occupy in the minds of your prospective clients can be a critical factor in their decision to meet with you or not. If you find that prospects are choosing to work with your competitors, you may need to reposition yourself against the competition. Try conducting some **competitive research** to find out what it is that clients like about the people you are competing with. Are those qualities you can emulate? In what areas are clients not as satisfied with them? Could you offer them more satisfaction there?

Start by asking your current or former clients about their experience with the competition. They may be quite candid with you about what they liked and didn't like, and also give you some valuable insight into why they chose you. To expand your research to prospective clients, you could approach them directly with your questions, but many won't want to answer. Consider hiring a market researcher to survey them for you. They may be much more willing to speak with a third party.

An easy way to check out how your competitors are positioning themselves without revealing what you're up to is surfing the Web. Mission statements, lists of features and benefits, and other valuable information will be posted on their websites. For more in-depth details, you can have a friend request their literature or hire a researcher to help.

Target market research may be another direction to look if prospects are telling you they don't need what you are offering. If you think they need a team-building retreat, but they think their problem can be solved with more skills training, you won't make a sale. When you learn more about how prospects view their own challenges, you can develop a **new market position** to match their mental, or real-life, purchase order better. Often just a change in language can alter how prospects view your offer. Your retreat just might fly if you described it as "an intensive three-day training program in the critical skills needed for effective teamwork."

Don't forget to ask current and former clients to help you position your services correctly. One way to discover how your market perceives the value in your work is to ask satisfied clients for a testimonial letter. The way they describe the work you do and benefits they received from it can give you valuable clues in how to sell it to others. An evaluation questionnaire can be used for the same purpose. Try asking, "How would you describe my service to someone else who could use it?"

It's also possible you will discover that you've chosen the wrong market; the perceived need for what you offer just isn't strong enough, they aren't willing to pay what you need to charge, or the size of the market is too limited. In this case, it's time to position yourself for an entirely different market. Make sure you do your homework on any possible new markets in advance, so you won't make the same mistake a second time.

A career counselor who is having a hard time finding individuals who will pay her fee can market herself to companies in need of outplacement services. A computer software trainer who discovers that large companies prefer working with training firms that can serve them on a national scale might find a better market in small to midsize organizations. Keep asking the question, "Who is most likely to hire me?" until you find the right fit.

Another problem your research might uncover is that your service isn't packaged in a way that prospects want to buy it. Developing a **better service package** could make what you offer more attractive. A marketing consultant who has been working on a project basis might find clients more receptive to a monthly retainer they can budget for. An interior designer encountering resistance to paying an hourly fee might instead raise his markup or commission on furnishings, and no longer charge by the hour at all.

Sometimes just naming your service package can make a difference. An image consultant might be much more successful selling the "One-Day Makeover" than suggesting to clients they buy six hours of her time to revamp their whole look. When doing your market research, try asking your prospects how they prefer to buy services like yours, and tailor your offering to their preferences.

One final roadblock you may be putting in your own way is offering too much. When someone asks exactly what it is that you do or specifically how you can help them, it really doesn't work to say, "I can do pretty much anything in the area of [fill in the blank]. What do you need?" It may be absolutely true that you can do almost anything in your field of expertise, but people don't buy "anything," they buy

Know Yourself and You'll Know Your Clients

"All the tips and tricks in the world don't work unless a business has a good service or product for which there is a market," contends Allison Bliss, a consultant who specializes in authentic marketing and communications for growing companies. "The number one reason businesses fail is that business owners don't determine whether there is a market for their products or services before they launch their business. Therefore, accurate market research is a key to successfully introducing, defining, positioning, packaging, and promoting your business.

"Why don't businesses do their research or conduct evaluations of their clients or customers? I find the bottom line reason is denial. Business owners may not want to hear the truth (good or bad) because they fear they may have to change something about their business. And people fear change, whether it advantages them or not."

Allison emphasizes that market research doesn't have to force you into an uncomfortable box: "I find increasingly often that if business owners position their businesses based on their own unique spirit or passion, they feel more comfortable in their marketing efforts. They derive a deeper and more meaningful experience by integrating their beliefs into their business, and become more successful over time in balancing the growth of the business with their lives. It becomes easier for their clients or customers to understand what they offer, and they begin to attract the customers they desire.

"In other words, instead of trying to be all things to all people—the most common marketing mistake I see among small businesses—the reality is that using your uniqueness in positioning and promoting a business will gain a better market share, and attract the clients with whom you want to conduct business."

Allison Bliss
www.allisonbliss.com

something specific. It's a rare prospect who will agree to meet with you just to share his problems and goals without knowing exactly what you are selling.

A **narrower focus of services** will allow prospects to have a better sense of how much they need you. It will also help them remember who you are. Having people know that you do "something with computers" will not lead to many inquiries or referrals. If they think of you instead as an expert in accounting and financial management software, you could find a place in their contact database.

Just as with choosing a market niche, don't worry that you are limiting yourself with this focus. Once you are in conversation with a prospect, you can propose other services that are within your range of expertise. But you need the narrower focus to get their attention so you can have the conversation in the first place.

Chapter 10

Closing Sales: When You're Making Appointments but Not Getting Sales

"When you get into a tight place and everything goes against you, till it seems as though you could not hold on a minute longer, never give up then, for that is just the place and time that the tide will turn."
—Harriet Beecher Stowe

The Final Frontier

To make your way to this final stage of the Universal Marketing Cycle, you've already done a lot of things right. You've identified good prospects, gotten up the nerve to contact them, and convinced them to meet with you. Getting stuck at this point, after investing a great deal of time and effort, can be really frustrating.

Understand first that some sales can't be made—or at least can't be made now. The vast majority of reasons that a prospect may choose to say no are completely out of your control. In fact, most consultants and professionals find that only one out of three prospects they present to will become a client. This means at least two out of three are saying no.

Many of the reasons prospects decide not to buy are standard objections you can attempt to handle, some of which are covered near the end of this chapter under "Making the Sale." Others, however, have more to do with how you are presenting and selling yourself. Since this *is* under your control, some suggestions for improvement follow. First we'll look at issues of credibility and then move on to specific techniques that you can use for your presentations.

Strategy: Networking and Referral Building,

 Public Speaking,

 Writing and Publicity,

 Promotional Events,

and

 Advertising

Success Ingredients

Professional credibility

Testimonials or references

RECIPE: *Building Your Credibility*

If you find that prospects tend to ask a lot of questions about your background and experience, increasing your **professional credibility** may help to make the sale go through. Using the marketing strategies of public speaking and writing and publicity are one way to do this. Networking in a professional association (yours or the prospect's) is another. Referral building activities focused on prominent center-of-influence people is a third.

Take a hard look at your credentials: work experience, formal education, speaking and publication credits, professional affiliations, and visible achievements. Based on what you see, would you hire yourself? Without a strong recommendation, prospects may be hesitant to do business with you if your credentials are light.

If it's experience you lack, consider donating your professional services to a community organization. If it's education, it might be time to earn a certificate in your specialty or take some more classes. Find other opportunities to add to your list of accomplishments and affiliations. Teach a class, organize a community or professional event, enter a contest, or seek out an award.

Then make sure you broadcast your credentials in all your marketing efforts. Cite the key accomplishments that make you credible in your Web copy, marketing materials, article bylines, or advertisements. Mention them when you speak or host a promotional event. It won't help you to acquire more credentials if people don't know about them.

A solid portfolio of **testimonials or references** can also convince

---

Answer the Questions Before They Are Asked

"Effective marketing techniques enable clients to find answers to the essential questions about your credibility before they meet you," claims Tom Lambert, chairman of the International Centre for Consulting Excellence. "What is more, some can be an excellent source of income. After twenty years of research and testing, we know what the profession's highest earners do to build and sustain their incomes. Do what *demonstrates* your skills, knowledge, and experience, and you will answer those key questions in advance.

"Write articles for those journals that your targeted prospects read. Invite contact by offering further information to those that request it.

"Conduct seminars and speak at conferences, giving the delegates useful information to take away that encourages them to make personal contact.

"Attend professional and trade meetings and network effectively.

"Conduct surveys and research to win press coverage, and comment on matters of current interest to the press in order to get your name into the papers, your voice on radio, and your face on television.

"Publish useful newsletters as a means of demonstrating your unique abilities and as a way of coming into contact with decision-makers in the industries that you serve.

"If you must, write a book.

"The top earners avoid anything that will be seen as mere 'promotional puffery,' but market consistently and make money directly from their marketing efforts where they can."

Tom Lambert, FRSA
www.icfce.com

prospects of your credibility. Include testimonial quotes on your website or brochure and testimonial letters in your marketing kit. The best testimonial letters are written directly to you ("Dear Karl, thank you so much for the contribution you have made to my success . . ."), rather than "To Whom It May Concern." Whenever clients tell you how happy they are with the service you are providing, ask if you can quote them. If your service needs to remain confidential, ask for an anonymous testimonial, and identify the client only by job title or city.

Testimonials or your client list are good to include in your marketing materials, but references should be available only by request. You don't want prospects calling your references before they decide to meet with you. Have a list of references ready, though, to offer after your presentation, if they ask. The more current your references are, the better, and be sure all the contact information is up-to-date.

Whether you let your references know who will be calling them is up to you, but definitely stay in touch with them as long as you continue to give out their names. When choosing who to use as a reference from many possibilities, focus on who can give the best confirmation of your capabilities. If those turn out to be the smaller or lesser-known clients, that's okay. You can still use any big names to head up your client list.

 **Strategy: Direct Contact and Follow-Up**

and

 Networking and Referral Building

Success Ingredients

Better-qualified prospects

Stronger relationships

Presentation script/visuals

Presentation skills

Portfolio

Leave-behind

Selling script

Selling skills

RECIPE: *Changing Who You Present To*

One of the ways to have more presentations turn into sales is to make fewer presentations—fewer, that is, to people who aren't qualified buyers. It's tempting to make a presentation to anyone who will listen, but that just takes up time you could have spent finding **better-qualified prospects**. Review the suggestions in Chapter 9 for developing qualifying questions and finding higher-quality leads and referrals to help with this goal.

Remember that the more people you can get to contact you, instead of you contacting them, the easier your selling task will be. Focusing more effort on professional visibility, generating referrals, and building a stickier website can help just as much in closing sales as it does in filling the pipeline and getting presentations.

Sometimes the main reason that presentations don't result in closed sales is that your prospects don't know you well enough yet. Consider spending more time building **stronger relationships** up front with the people you wish to present to. Attend networking meetings, conferences, or social events that your prospects frequent, or invite them to events you plan to attend. Schedule coffee, lunch, or a date to play tennis or golf to get better acquainted. Send your prospects articles and other information that will help them do their jobs better or achieve their personal goals. Or follow some of the suggestions in Chapter 9 to identify personal connections that already exist between you, or find a mutual contact to put in a good word on your behalf.

A primary reason that people hire a professional services provider is to serve as an expert resource. Look for ways to serve your prospects before selling to them. Give them tastes of your expertise and the resources at your disposal in all your marketing materials, on your website, at speaking engagements, in your newsletter, and any other way they come in contact with you. Often this will result in prospects becoming clients without either of you having to work at it.

RECIPE: *Scripting Your Presentations*

For each sales presentation, you should be prepared with a **presentation script**, whether you will be presenting in person or over the phone. Like a telemarketing script, this is actually a series of talking points, rather than something you memorize and repeat. Here's a general outline:

1. *Establish rapport.* Introduce yourself, make sure you know with whom you are speaking and who else is in the room. When presenting in

person, chat about whatever sequence of events got you there or something else you all have in common.

2. *Determine their needs.* Begin by repeating what you already know, and then start asking questions. Your script should include all the questions you must have an answer to in order to write a proposal or close the deal on the spot. Open-ended questions will elicit more information than those that can be answered with a yes or no. Many questions will be specific to your line of business, but here are some typical ones:

- What is your current situation?
- How important or urgent is it that you solve this problem?
- What have you already tried?
- When do you need this done, or when were you thinking about getting started?
- What resources do you already have lined up?
- What other solutions are you considering?
- What would the perfect solution look like?
- What kind of budget do you have, or what were you expecting to pay?

3. *Explain how you can meet their needs.* Using the information you have just gathered, respond to each problem or goal they mentioned by describing how you can help. Use specific examples to illustrate your explanation—for example, "My last client had exactly the same challenge, and what I did for her was . . ."

4. *Answer their questions.* Find out how you are doing by asking, "What else do you need to know?" Keep asking for and answering questions until they seem satisfied. Address any concerns that come up, one by one. Reassure them that you are the right solution to their problem by responding specifically with how you can help.

5. *Ask for the business.* Don't leave this step out. Even if you know they will want to see a proposal first, are talking to other people, or aren't ready to make a decision, ask anyway. It's the only way you will find out how close you are to making a sale. Whatever they say in response to this question will tell you exactly what you need to resolve before your prospects will buy.

6. *Decide on a next step.* Whether or not you have closed the sale, be absolutely certain that both you and the prospect know what happens next. Is she ready to get started? When? Will there be a contract or purchase order involved? Who has to sign off on it? Does she need a written proposal? Does she want to check your references? Can you call back in a week? If you don't already know, find out if she will be talking to other people before making a decision. And be sure to ask if there is anything you can do to help move things forward.

If you use a free sample of your services as a sales strategy, such as a complimentary consultation or sample session, don't allow the sample to completely replace your sales presentation. Although many of the questions you might normally ask during a presentation may be covered during the course of your complimentary session, you will still need to connect the dots for your prospect between what he needs and what you do. Don't assume he will figure that out by himself just from his brief experience of working with you. You will also still need to ask for the sale. Be sure to leave enough time at the conclusion of your session for these important aspects of selling.

Once you have developed and mastered the content of your sales presentation, consider whether your **presentation skills** may also need some improvement. For one-on-one presentations, work on your questioning and listening abilities. When you present to groups of people, your speaking skills become more important. Take a workshop, hire a coach, or join a group to gain more practice in presenting.

These suggestions for presenting assume that your presentation is taking place interactively, in person or by phone. But it is sometimes possible to "present" by e-mail. While this is not typically the most effective approach, some prospects may lead you into an e-mail presentation by e-mailing you with detailed questions about how you work and what you charge before they are willing to speak with you live.

When you find yourself in this situation, take care that you have learned enough about your prospect's needs to adequately explain how you can meet them. You may need to ask additional questions of your own before responding with all the details your prospect has requested. If you don't take this step, your generic response may be a poor match for her requirements and you won't get a second chance to present what you can do.

Make a Connection and You'll Make the Sale

"Pay attention to what others say as they say it. Don't formulate your response while they are speaking. Just listen." That's the advice of communications consultant Patricia Haddock, author of eleven books and over 600 magazine articles. Here are some of her tips for more powerful presentations.

"1. *Use stories and anecdotes* to illustrate your points and involve your listeners. People relate to other people; storytelling captures the imagination and the memory.

"2. *Rehearse.* Each time you rehearse your presentation—whether physically or going over it in your mind—you program it into your brain and body. The more familiar you are with the material, the more natural you will sound.

"3. *Make continuous eye contact* to draw your listeners to you and keep their attention. Express interest by nodding, making eye contact, and smiling.

"4. *Read audience body language* to make sure you are keeping their attention. If you see glazed looks, crossed arms, or blank stares, pick up the pace, move around, ask questions, tell a story, or cut to a key benefit that will wake them up.

"5. *Ask open-ended questions* that require more than simple yes or no answers. Require straightforward answers to your questions. Rephrase your question until the person responds appropriately.

"6. *Paraphrase* what the other person says, and ask if you are interpreting his or her comments correctly.

"7. *Ask for what you want*, and if you hear no, start negotiating."

Patricia Haddock
www.patriciahaddock.com

RECIPE: *Adding Tangibility to Your Presentations*

Services are intangible; they can't be seen or touched like a product can. Consider supporting your presentation's talking points with some **presentation visuals**. In person, topics outlined on a flipchart or laptop screen, diagrams, illustrations, and photographs can help give what you have to say more weight. When presenting by phone, the same material can be displayed on the Web or e-mailed to your prospect in advance, so the two of you can review it together.

Another solution is to provide a **portfolio** of your best work. Artists, designers, and other professionals who create tangible objects routinely do this, but in fact, anyone can. Your portfolio could be available online, or you can bring a portfolio with you to an in-person meeting. You might include samples of your writing, reports you have prepared, project schedules, program outlines, or action photos of you at work. Going through your portfolio with a prospect, or flipping to a certain page as questions arise, can further establish your expertise.

While a portfolio is something you and a prospect often review together, the purpose of a **leave-behind** is to give your prospects a sample of your work they can hang on to or a gift to remember you by. A leave-behind that serves as a sample could be a case study, special report, before-and-after photos, or a collection of testimonials. Gift leave-behinds include books, audios, mousepads, coffee cups, or even candy. You can also mail or e-mail your leave-behind after a phone presentation. The idea is to give your prospect a present they will use or refer to, and therefore continue to think of you.

RECIPE: *Making the Sale*

If you're doing your job right, the selling begins before the presentation ends. The moment you begin explaining exactly how your services can solve the prospect's problem, you are starting to sell. So what's the difference between a **selling script** and a presentation script? Not too much. But if you find yourself doing fine until it's time to ask for the business and then you start floundering, a better selling script is what you need.

Asking for the business can feel a bit confronting. This is the moment in your presentation when you are most likely to be rejected, so you may find yourself resisting asking a direct question to find out whether you have the sale. Keep in mind that your prospect is expecting this question. He knows this is a sales situation and at some point you are going to request his agreement to go forward. So don't back away from asking directly. You will leave your prospect hanging, and the future of your sale uncertain.

Up until this moment in the presentation, you have been asking mostly open-ended questions to gather as much information as possible and keep all possibilities open. Now you should switch to a yes or no question. What this form of question will do is elicit three possible answers: yes, no, or the reason why not. The good news is that prospects almost never say no. Instead, they respond with a specific reason why they aren't saying yes just yet. And this is exactly the information you need to make the sale.

There are many different ways to ask your prospect for the business. Here are some sample questions that might be in your selling script:

"Are you ready to get started?"

"Would you like to schedule an appointment?"

"Shall I draw up a contract?"

"Would you like to sign up?"

"Is my proposal acceptable?"

"Shall I finalize the details?"

"Do we have a deal?"

The most important element of asking for the business is to ask your closing question and then shut up! Don't talk yourself out of a sale by saying, "Is my proposal acceptable or is the price too high? I know you had some concerns about the budget and . . ." Wait to hear whether your prospect has any objections, and if so, what they are. Even if the silence starts to get uncomfortable, don't speak until your prospect answers you.

The next words out of your prospect's mouth will tell you exactly what you need to hear. It's likely to be an objection. This doesn't mean you have lost the sale. In fact, it may mean you have made it. "Well, it's a lot of money to spend," is not a real objection; it's probably a statement of fact. An appropriate response might be, "You're right, it's quite an investment. What do you think, are you ready to take the plunge?"

Real objections, though, need to be overcome—or to reframe this in a way you might find more helpful, they are "considerations that need to be resolved," or "points that need to be handled," in order for the sale to go through. Include in your selling script all the typical objections people in your line of work encounter, and some possible responses to each one.

Never disagree with a prospect's objections or try to argue with them. Instead, validate what your prospect is saying and reassure her that the two of you will work together to find a solution that serves you both. Once your prospect hires you, you will be working together on many solutions, and what better time to start? Maintain a friendly, helpful, service-oriented attitude, and you will find selling conversations to be much more comfortable than if you become defensive or adversarial.

Remember, too, that once you leave the room or hang up the phone, you may find yourself back in voice mail limbo. For that reason, it's wise to make every possible use of this opportunity to deal with your prospect's considerations person-to-person.

The best way to respond to an objection is to agree completely with what your prospect is saying, then ask another open-ended question that leads the conversation back to how your service can be of value. Here are some examples:

The prospect says . . .	*You respond . . .*
We can't afford to spend that much.	Yes, I know the price is significant. Let me ask you, what is it costing you not to fix it?
I need to think about it.	It's a big decision, and I'm sure you do. Tell me, what are some of your concerns?
I'm not sure it will help.	Yes, I understand you can't know that until we get started. If it did help, what might you get out of it?
We're too busy right now.	I know how busy you are. Tell me, if you don't deal with the situation now, when will you be less busy?
It's too expensive.	Yes, it's a big investment. What results would make that kind of investment worthwhile?
We're not ready.	I understand that you have a lot going on. What will need to change in order for you to be ready?
I'm not sure you're right for the job.	Yes, I know that you may have concerns about that. What would you need to feel confident about in order to hire me?

When your prospect replies to the new question you have asked, treat his response as one more need he has expressed, and explain how you

---

To Win More Sales, Try Being Honest

"People buy from people they trust," emphasizes Gill E. Wagner, author of *Honest Selling: How to Build the [Your Name Here] Sales System* (Café Press, 2004). "If you do anything in a sales situation that leads the prospect to distrust you, your odds of closing the sale become virtually zero. The only chance an untrustworthy salesperson has of closing the deal is if all the other salespeople are also unworthy of trust. The person who is distrusted the least will get the sale.

"You can't create profound trust in a few minutes. Everything you've ever been taught about creating deeply felt trust in only minutes is garbage, unless the words 'a million' preceded 'minutes.' Deeply felt trust is earned over time, not stolen by employing some interview tactic. Do you want to be trusted? Then be trustworthy all the time.

"Sales resistance does *not* naturally exist in the selling process. The actions you take during the sales conversation will either create sales resistance or stop it from occurring. The trick to eliminating sales resistance is to always keep the prospect's best interests in mind. That way, even when you challenge his or her thinking—because you honestly believe a mistake is being made—you will maintain a collaborative relationship and avoid sales resistance.

"Karma, chemistry, and commonality have little to do with sales success. Yes, there are instances in which two people simply don't 'click.' But the idea that someone won't buy from you unless you have the type of chemistry that creates lifetime best friends is ludicrous. If you want to make 'chemistry' irrelevant, simply be honest."

Gill E. Wagner
www.honestselling.com

---

can meet it. If you still believe that your service is the best solution your prospect could find, keep asking questions until you have uncovered and responded to as many objections as you can. Then ask for the business again and see what happens.

If at any point in the presentation you discover some concrete reasons why your service would not be a good fit for your prospect's needs, tell him so, and gracefully end the appointment. Recommend another provider who might be a better solution, if you know one. There's no value to either of you in trying to close a sale that will ultimately end in you taking a job you won't enjoy, or your client not being satisfied.

If every presentation seems to get bogged down with objections at the end, you are probably asking for the business too soon. Try asking, "What concerns do you have?" before introducing a closing question. That way you can work to resolve those concerns while you are still in the more comfortable phase of open conversation, and don't yet feel so pressured to sell.

Learning to do a good job at this kind of high-stakes verbal exchange may require improving your **selling skills**. Books and audio programs can help, but significant improvement will take practice. Workshops and other group environments are one way, or you can role-play with a friend or coach. One of the biggest obstacles to successful selling is lack of self-confidence, and that's what practice in a safe environment will help to build.

RECIPE: *Following Up*

When you don't make the sale at the time of the presentation, you haven't yet lost it. But if you don't follow up, you probably will. Everyone who has been in business for any length of time has a story about a sale that finally went through eighteen months after the presentation or after the eleventh follow-up call. Once you have made contact with a prospect who needs you, can pay you, and already knows what you can do for them, don't let them go!

Contact your prospects at regular intervals, using all the methods described in Chapter 8. Be friendly, considerate, and professional, but be persistent. If they really don't want to hear from you, they will tell you. Until then, keep following up.

A Final Word About Fear

The moment of truth in a selling conversation is when you ask for the business. As soon as you ask the question, you run the risk of being turned down. The thought of that can be so scary that you stop yourself from asking, maybe not even consciously. You walk out of the meeting or hang up the phone, and realize that you still don't know whether the prospect will buy.

To become successful at selling, you must overcome this last self-imposed obstacle. Try a memory jogger first. When presenting by phone,

The Doorway to Freedom

"Fear is the gatekeeper of your comfort zone," counsels Rhonda Britten, author of *Fearless Living* (Dutton, 2001). "Your comfort zone is whatever is familiar to you. As a little child, your comfort zone was your mother's lap. You ventured away out of curiosity but scurried back to safety when you felt threatened. Now your comfort zone is the people you already know, the routines you're used to, the places where you feel at home. Whether these are bad, good, happy, or sad is immaterial. As the old saying goes, 'Better the devil you know than the devil you don't know.'

"But how satisfying is safe? Fear keeps us from feeling alive when there's a danger of not being accepted, approved, or understood. Therefore we deny our essential nature. Fear doesn't know you are an adult who craves adventure and love and fulfillment. It doesn't know that you could handle it from here. That is why a crisis is sometimes what's necessary to shake up your world and give you the courage you need to show your fear who's boss.

"There is almost certainly some level of crisis manifesting itself in your life right now. Maybe you are simply sick of letting yourself down or listening to your own excuses. Perhaps you've had enough of never finding the courage to stand up for yourself. Maybe you are tired of not earning what you're worth just because you can't bring yourself to put a real value on your contribution. You may not even be able to pinpoint what's going on but you know something isn't quite working. Your soul yearns for more. That's all you need to get started on the journey from fear to freedom."

Rhonda Britten
www.fearlessliving.org

post a sign bearing your favorite closing question where you can't avoid seeing it. For in-person presentations, you may need to be more subtle. Stick a note inside your calendar, note pad, or card case and leave it open in your lap.

If you still find yourself choking on the closing question, start by asking something more indirect. At the point in the presentation where the prospect has no more questions, ask, "Where are we?" or "What's our next step?" This may give you all the information you need to uncover any objections before moving forward. Then it may feel safe enough to ask a more direct question to see if you have the sale.

Practice asking closing questions with a friend or coach. Trust that the more you ask, the more confident you will become. And remember that the only way you are likely to get anything you want in life is to ask for it.

Index